A PORTRAIT OF PROSPERITY

Vancouver

Produced in cooperation with the
Greater Vancouver Chamber of Commerce
Photo by Cliff Barbour

The Greater Vancouver Chamber of Commerce and Community Communications, Inc.,
would like to express our gratitude to these companies for their leadership in the development of this book.

A PORTRAIT OF PROSPERITY

Vancouver

By Jane Elder Wulff
Corporate profiles by K.C. Cowan
Featuring the photography of Cliff C. Barbour

Community Communications, Inc.
Publisher: Ronald P. Beers

Staff for *Vancouver: A Portrait of Prosperity*

Acquisitions	*Henry S. Beers*
Publisher's Sales Associate	*Marlene Berg*
Editor in Chief	*Wendi L. Lewis*
Managing Editor	*Amy Newell*
Profile Editor	*Amanda J. Burbank*
Design Director	*Scott Phillips*
Designer	*Eddie Lavoie*
Photo Editors	*Eddie Lavoie and Amy Newell*
Contract Manager	*Christi Stevens*
National Sales Manager	*Ronald P. Beers*
Sales Assistant	*Sandra Akers*
Acquisitions Coordinator	*Angela P. White*
Proofreader	*Allison L. Griffin*
Accounting Services	*Stephanie Perez*
Print Production Manager	*Jarrod Stiff*
Pre-Press and Separations	*Artcraft Graphic Productions*

Community Communications, Inc.
Montgomery, Alabama

David M. Williamson, Chief Executive Officer
Ronald P. Beers, President
W. David Brown, Chief Operating Officer

© 2000 Community Communications
All Rights Reserved
Published 2000
Printed in U.S.A.
First Edition
Library of Congress Catalog Number: 00-010340
ISBN: 1-58192-028-8

Every effort has been made to ensure the accuracy of the information herein.
However, the authors and Community Communications are not responsible
for any errors that might have occurred.

Table of Contents

Chapter 1
THE RIVER SHAPES A COMMUNITY, 14

Like countless earlier generations, the people of Vancouver and Clark County prosper in the mighty embrace of the Columbia River. Its fertile soil nourishes a dynamic community of pioneer descendants and newcomers working together—as the region grows by leaps and bounds—to sustain the good life that brings all these people here. The Columbia River Renaissance partnership is a giant step toward realizing this shared vision.

Chapter 2
THE GIFT OF KNOWLEDGE, 28

A strong educational system attracts new businesses to Vancouver and Clark County, advancing opportunities for employees and improving their families' quality of life. Local businesses, recognizing education's crucial role, give back abundantly in partnerships with schools, school districts, Clark College, and the southwest Washington branch of Washington State University. Dozens of smaller programs meet specific educational needs in the community.

Chapter 3
A FOUNDATION FOR GROWTH, 36

Vancouver and Clark County citizens have launched their community's economic leap into the future from a sound footing in history. Cultural treasures of the Northwest's oldest neighborhood stand proudly beside handsome new developments designed with a local sense of place and purpose. River-based high-tech manufacturing and marine transportation anchor a richly diverse and burgeoning local economy, with one of the highest employment rates in the nation.

Chapter 4
A SPIRIT OF UNITY, 44

Named "the Friendly Reach" by early explorers to honor Chinook generosity, this stretch of river shoreline still hosts a tradition of friendliness. As new neighborhoods blossom and old ones thrive, Vancouver's city-sponsored network of neighborhood associations helps keep them connected. In Clark County, too, and in its smaller cities, long-established neighborhood networks are sprouting new associations. The result is a continuing legacy of community pride.

Chapter 5
A COMMUNITY THAT CARES, 52

A sense of sharing and stewardship pervades Vancouver and Clark County communities. From foundations and service groups to family benefactors and individual volunteers, people here look out for each other. Premier health care is an important part of the picture, while partnerships to preserve environmental and historical resources provide models for the nation.

Chapter 6
RECREATION & CELEBRATIONS, 62

Nature fashioned an idyllic setting for Vancouver and Clark County, amid green fields and hills, forests, streams, lakes, and mountains. Making the most of nature's gifts, residents have created urban trail systems, parks and greenways, sports complexes, and wildlife sanctuaries. Take your pick: a Volcanic Monument one way, ocean beaches another, or history and music, art and theater, fairs, festivals, and the Vancouver Farmers Market here at home.

Chapter 7
A REGIONAL IDENTITY, 72

Vancouver and Clark County residents appreciate their close-knit community, steeped in small-town character, all the more for the richness and variety that surrounds it—from big-city amenities and an international airport right across the water to a wealth of natural wonders on all sides. They relish their active role in a region that leads the world in meeting the economic, environmental, and human imperatives of the new millennium.

Chapter 8
FOCUS ON THE FUTURE, 82

Clark is one of the fastest-growing counties in the nation. Housing and educating the populace, moving them from place to place, and maintaining their quality of life are tremendous challenges in this climate of growth. While citizens roll up their sleeves, a new central city rises to complete Vancouver's river renaissance, setting the scene for its role in the nationwide Lewis and Clark Bicentennial Commemoration.

Chapter 9

TRANSPORTATION, ENERGY, & COMMUNICATIONS, 94

Bonneville Power Administration, 96
Tidewater Barge Lines, Inc., 98
Ray Hickey: Hickey Family Company, 100
New Edge Networks, 102
Vancouver Business Journal, 104

Chapter 10

TECHNOLOGY, MANUFACTURING, & DISTRIBUTION, 106

Sharp, 108
Underwriters Laboratories Inc. of Camas, 110
Boise Cascade, 112
WaferTech, 114
Kyocera Industrial Ceramics Corporation, 115
ConAgra Malt: Great Western Malting Company, 116

Chapter 11

THE BUSINESS COMMUNITY, 118

Greater Vancouver Chamber of Commerce, 120
Columbia Credit Union, 122
LSW Architects, P.C., 124
West Coast Bank, 126
Design Showroom, Inc., 127
Lacamas Community Credit Union, 128
Clark County School Employees Credit Union, 129

Chapter 12

REAL ESTATE, DEVELOPMENT, & CONSTRUCTION, 130

Norris, Beggs & Simpson, 132
Century 21 Complete Realty, 133
Tapani Underground, 134
North Coast Electric Company, 135
Otak and Killian Pacific, 136

FOREWORD, 8
PREFACE, 10

PART ONE, 12
PART TWO, 92

ENTERPRISE INDEX, 154
BIBLIOGRAPHY, 156
INDEX, 157
PATRONS, 160

Chapter 13

HEALTH CARE, 138

Southwest Washington Medical Center, 140
Wendel Family Dental Centre, 144
The Vancouver Clinic, 145
Kaiser Permanente, 146

Chapter 14

EDUCATION, 148

Clark College, 150
Clark County's Educational Community, 152

Photos by Cliff Barbour

Vancouver

FOREWORD

It is my pleasure on behalf of the Greater Vancouver Chamber of Commerce to introduce Vancouver and Clark County in *A Portrait of Prosperity*. As you will see in these pages, a robust economy and a thriving business environment are just part of the prosperity we enjoy in this community. Yes, this is a region of unmatched historical resources, beautiful mountains and rivers, a great climate—but the true mark of our prosperity, the one invaluable asset that pulls it all together, is our *human* resources.

Our people, wherever they sit at the table, have always shown a collective willingness to work together for a better quality of life. We are facing the challenges of a new century—unprecedented growth, globalization, technological change—in this same spirit of collaboration. Diverse interests in the community approach tough challenges in various ways, but a strong shared belief in partnership continues to bring these groups together to shape a common vision.

Above all, we share a strong commitment to our young people—our most important resource. Here in Vancouver and Clark County, we understand that what's good for children, families, neighborhoods, schools, and communities is good for business. Here, prosperity is more than just a word. We're making our vision real, together.

—*Doug Maas*
President and Chief Executive Officer
Greater Vancouver Chamber of Commerce

A Portrait of Prosperity

PREFACE

In the beginning of a project like this, no one knows exactly what the final result will be. Going on faith, hundreds of people all over Vancouver and Clark County were answering my calls, telling me their part of the story and trusting me to put it to good use.

Everything they told me reinforced the guiding theme of a river heritage being borne by many hands into the future. As each piece of the story found its place and I watched the whole tapestry taking shape, I became more and more excited. The people living this story knew what they were bringing to it, but they could not yet see how it all fit together. Now they will be able to share my excitement, and for that I am grateful.

This is their story, and their trust and willingness to be part of it have made it what it is. Their voices are all here, quoted or not, named or not. Voices from the past are here too, not relegated to a separate chapter but woven in among our daily lives—and if you listen closely, you can hear voices from the future, full of welcome and praise for a job well done.

My personal thanks to Christina Demetro, for her inspiration and encouragement; to Jim and Eva Demetro, for their talent, generosity, and warmth; to Royce Pollard, for his bravehearted devotion to Vancouver's history and promise; to Rhonda Carey, Bill Fromhold, Doug Maas, and everyone at the Chamber who helped the project along; to Amy Newell, who made the editorial process a joy; and to Gina Bacon, who opened this door for me.

—*Jane Elder Wulff*

Photo by Cliff Barbour

PART ONE

A Portrait of Prosperity

The River Shapes a Community

Chapter 1

When we reached the garrison and I had a good view of the grand old Columbia River and the snowclad peaks ... I felt as if I could battle with the pioneer life of a new country.

—Delia B. Sheffield, 17-year-old Army wife, arriving in Vancouver in September, 1852

The Columbia River links the people of Clark County to their past and future. Photos by Cliff Barbour

(above) *Photo by Cliff Barbour*

Vancouver lies cradled in a broad bend of the westering Columbia River, where it turns northward one last time on its way to the sea. As the flow of water has shaped the land, so has the river always shaped this community.

Here were the Wapato Lowlands, ancestral home of the river people known as the Chinook—one of the most densely populated regions on the continent before Euro-American settlement. Here, British fur traders and Yankee soldiers came and went by water, forging from their practical peace what has been called the Northwest's oldest neighborhood. Here the river continues to sustain us in countless ways, making us who we are and who we will be, far into the future. Today and tomorrow, it is our turn to be the river people and our shared vision to be worthy of that heritage.

* * *

The blind clay figure of Captain George Vancouver stands head and shoulders above its creator, sculptor Jim Demetro. Questing, leaning forward, the great explorer and cartographer offers one hand as if in welcome, holding in the other a rolled map. Fourth-graders press in close, warming lumps of clay between their palms, while environmental educator Christina Demetro, Jim's daughter and an artist in her own right, encourages them to take their time.

"Pick a spot on the statue that you'll remember," she says. "Then years from now, when you bring your families back to see the monument, you can tell them, 'That's my spot! That's where I helped sculpt the statue of Captain Vancouver!'"

For six weeks in the spring of 1999, the Demetros welcomed the public to an improvised sculpting gazebo in the courtyard of the new City Center 12 Cinemas in downtown Vancouver. Center developer Elie Kassab offered to match funds, and Friends of Vancouver, the nonprofit group created to support the project, hired Jim Demetro to design and execute the work.

Jim and Christina made substantial donations of time and invited citizens to help. For a dollar, you could add a bit of clay to the statue.

For $20 you could get a certificate signed by Mayor Royce Pollard and have your name engraved on the Contributors' Plaque. Schoolchildren, of course, could sculpt for free.

"It was the mayor who started it," said Avril Massey, then president of the local Daughters of the British Empire, later founder of the Friends. "He heard the DBE was sending money for a statue in King's Lynn, Norwich, England, the captain's birthplace. He marched into my tearoom and said, 'Never mind the Brits! How about having a statue here?'"

Some people wondered why George Vancouver should be honored, since he never set foot here. Why not his lieutenant, William Broughton, who first charted the river in October 1792 and named this point of land for his captain? Better yet, why not the American Captain Robert Gray, the river's true discoverer, who had crossed its fearsome bar aboard the *Columbia Rediviva* almost under Vancouver's nose five months earlier?

Indeed, once he knew it was there, why did Captain Vancouver himself never enter the fabled River of the West? Having come so close, how could he resist? Such questions don't trouble Avril Massey: "Without the skipper, none of those others would have made it, either. He had other things on his mind. It's the chief executive with the vision who runs the company, you know."

Today's visionaries, like their namesake captain, face the challenge of uncharted territory, but they're not working in isolation. Partnerships as numerous as the hands that have shaped his statue

(above) Sculptor Jim Demetro adds details to the clay figure of Captain George Vancouver.

(below) Creating the statue of Captain Vancouver involved a collaborative community effort. From left, Jim Demetro, his wife, Eva, and their daughter, Christina, pose with the clay figure. Photos by Cliff Barbour

17

Reenactors lead visitors on a trip through time at Fort Vancouver, above, and Pomeroy Living History Farm.

are bringing new life to long-held dreams. Among the most stunning of these is the Columbia River Renaissance—a collaboration of dozens of public and private partners working to bring a 12-mile stretch of riverfront back into the community's daily life.

Following the pattern of most river cities, Vancouver grew up perceiving its waterway as strictly an industrial resource. Why else build a city by a river? Canoes carried beaver, seal, and otter furs to Fort Vancouver, established in 1825 as headquarters for the Hudson's Bay Company's vast Columbia District. Ships carried bales of furs away to England. Shipping and shipbuilding picked up steam, literally, after the U.S. Army established an American presence on the bluff above the fort in 1849.

That same year, the Hudson's Bay Company moved its district headquarters to Canada and began phasing out operations at Fort Vancouver. The Army base became the nucleus of what was already a diverse and thriving community. But while Portland's pioneers, across the Columbia in Oregon, were building a fine harbor in a sheltered tributary called the Willamette, the town of Vancouver remained a kind of military castle village and trade center. One of its earliest industries was a brewery. By 1880 it had 1500 residents and 10 saloons, more than any other kind of business.

Mechanization brought sawmills and paper mills to the river's north shore. Late in the century, Vancouver even ran a local railroad for a few years to bring the riches of field and forest down to the docks. It was far easier to travel the unbridled river by shallow-draft steamboat (which some said could navigate on fresh dew) than to hack across country.

Industry mushroomed along the waterfront as bridges opened Vancouver to Portland by rail in 1910, by road in 1917. In 1912 the city formed its own port. In both world wars, it served as a major shipbuilding center. Traditionally anchored in marine transportation, its economy has also depended on manufacturing processes that need unlimited water to make things like aluminum, silicon carbide, and wood products (and, more recently, high-tech components).

These developments buried the bank in wharves, warehouses, and equipment. By the time the 1917 bridge was twinned in the 1950s to accommodate the new interstate freeway, most Vancouver citizens had lost touch with their river—but not all. Within a decade, private investors had begun taking the first risky steps back to the shoreline, building restaurants near the bridge. Then came the first small waterfront park.

Finally, in the mid-1980s, public spirit coalesced around a vision of an unbroken riverfront serving the various needs of the entire community—an incomparable asset, a return to Vancouver's unique historical identity, and a leap into the future. In 1993 this vision received the National Waterfront Center's annual Award for Excellence.

A Portrait of Prosperity

(top) A Chinook fisherman was photographed in 1897 by Benjamin A. Gifford along the Columbia River.

(above) In the mid-1800s the Hudson's Bay Company occupied buildings like these reconstructions at Fort Vancouver.
Photos courtesy of Vancouver National Historic Reserve Trust

Troops carrying supplies assemble on Officers Row in the early 1900s. Photo courtesy of Vancouver National Historic Reserve Trust

(above) In the 1880s big-leaf maple trees had recently been planted along Officers Row. Present-day Marshall House is in center and Grant House is on far left. Photo courtesy of Vancouver National Historic Reserve Trust

(below) A reenactor, dressed in 19th-century military costume, stands watch at the square in Officers Row.

Many achievements later, the vision keeps gaining substance, piece by piece. In discussions for this story, no one person or agency or group takes the credit, but all are eager to credit others. Diverse as they are, they share certain experiences. They have let go of exclusive claims in order to work together. They have given ground for the common good and have felt the dynamic momentum of collaboration take hold. This is the essence of partnership, in this place, at this time, and the Columbia River Renaissance is just one of many examples to be set forth in detail in these pages.

Our community's gift for partnership springs from long tradition. When President Thomas Jefferson asked his private secretary to lead the search for the Northwest Passage, Meriwether Lewis could have kept the glory for himself. Instead, he insisted that his old comrade-at-arms, William Clark, share his command.

Homeward bound in the spring of 1806, after a wet winter miserably huddled near an ocean that was anything but pacific, the Corps of Discovery made camp on "a beautifull prarie" above the river. On the evening of March 30, Lewis wrote in his journal that with proper cultivation, the land around Point Vancouver could sustain "40 to 50 thousand souls." It was "the only desirable situation for a settlement" that he had seen west of the Rockies.

That settlement, later named Clark County after Lewis's partner, now sustains an estimated 337,000 souls, with more arriving every day. As Vancouver casts an ever-wider net, small towns that were once half a day's wagon ride away are growing to meet it. Fields that

(above) Workers prepare the statue of Captain Vancouver for its journey up the Columbia River.

(below) Well-wishers greet the statue as it arrives in Vancouver aboard the **Lady Washington.** *Photos by Cliff Barbour*

once supported dairy cows and hay, orchards and berries, now support houses and families. Clark is one of the fastest-growing counties in the nation, with more rural land for residential expansion than the Portland metropolitan area's three Oregon counties combined. The face of our community is changing quickly. In partnerships throughout the county and the region, we are working hard to ensure that it changes for the better.

Sometimes, though, we have to stop and celebrate. On the last Saturday in April, at the very beginning of the new century, a larger-than-life bronze statue sailed upstream on the deck of the *Lady Washington*, a working replica of the *Columbia Rediviva's* sister ship. After 200 years, Captain George Vancouver, with an escort led by Mayor Royce Pollard, was finally coming up the Columbia River to the city that bears his name.

No longer blind, the captain's smiling eyes now gleamed with clear vision. The map in his right hand had unfurled in a sheet of bronze. His welcoming left hand pointed to a bronze globe showing his route from England. Standing alone in the twilight, he seemed to see past the dedication ceremonies, the cheers, toasts, and speeches, to a world awaiting discovery. After all, uncharted territory was his specialty.

Vancouver

Bonneville Power Administration

Dependable energy is a sure sign of a sophisticated, urban community, and the BPA provides that and more. A leader in the Clark County area, it serves about eight million people—80 percent of the Northwest's population.

Operating more than 15,000 miles of high-voltage lines and moving nearly 26 billion watts of power, the BPA is sure to be a major player in the future of America's energy, as the Federal Energy Regulatory Commission forms Regional Transmission Organizations across the country. And it is the employees of the Vancouver-based Transmission Business Line and Dittmer Control Center who are responsible for operating, building, and maintaining these high-voltage electrical lines and substations. These capable and dedicated employees have proven time and again that the BPA can and will continue to provide residents of the Northwestern United States with affordable electricity and prompt and reliable service.

Clark College

One of Washington State's largest community and technical colleges, Clark College offers one- or two-year certificate programs for technical careers, two-year associate degrees in both technical and professional majors, and coursework to meet general education requirements for those students wishing to transfer to a four-year university. It is the college of choice for many Vancouver residents, offering affordable tuition, small classes, and flexible class scheduling.

Clark understands the power of cooperation. It partners with the business community by offering advanced training for current employees of area businesses; other colleges and universities, ensuring that its students undergo a smooth transition to a four-year institution; and local high schools, helping to avoid duplicate coursework and awarding hardworking students. Clark College is an unmistakable asset to the Vancouver area, touching the lives of its people and fueling its economy and workforce.

Sharp

Sharp, a world-renowned high-tech enterprise, brings its most recent innovations into every American home, through its Sharp Microelectronics of the Americas and Sharp Labs of America headquarters in Camas, Washington. It prides itself on the vision and ability of its southwest Washington employees who work as a team, challenging themselves and each other to anticipate and create products that will make people's lives easier.

For example, Sharp has been a world leader in Liquid Crystal Display (LCD) development for almost 30 years. Its LCD technology has not only made laptop computers lighter, clearer, and more energy efficient, but it is also a key component in flat-panel televisions, hand-held digital video appliances, cell phones, and other useful products that have changed the way Americans live and work. Sharp is a forward-thinking, creative company, dedicated to making a difference in people's lives. It knows that the products of the future are only a dream away.

Southwest Washington Medical Center

Southwest Washington Medical Center (SWMC) is the leading health-care provider in Clark County. As one of only six hospitals in the nation to have earned three Top 100 Hospital designations, SWMC is nationally recognized as a facility providing exceptional, comprehensive care. The national health-care research firm HCIA-Sachs ranked SWMC among America's 100 Top Hospitals in three categories: overall, orthopedics, and cardiovascular services.

An integrated health system with eight locations, SWMC meets the community's health needs in outpatient and inpatient diagnostic, medical, and surgical services. Nearly 2,800 staff and 400 doctors provide sophisticated and complex medical and surgical procedures supported by the best equipment that technology has to offer.

With wisdom and foresight that have carried it from the mid-1800s into this new millennium, SWMC has embraced a master plan for expanding services and facilities to meet the needs of a growing community.

A Portrait of Prosperity

The Gift of Knowledge

Chapter 2

School helps you learn how to solve problems, whether it's math or personal. You learn to think about your possibilities, things you can do. It all comes down to helping kids be whatever we want to be, so we can learn to help our community.

—Tanner Perkins, fourth grade
Captain Strong Elementary, Battle Ground
September, 2000

(above) *Clark College serves the educational needs of nearly 12,000 students. Photo courtesy of Clark Community College*

(left) *The college's Lewis D. Cannell Library contains a collection of more than 55,000 volumes. Photo by Cliff Barbour*

E ducation and business joined forces in Vancouver right from the start, when Chief Factor John McLoughlin hired schoolteachers for the children of diverse tribes and nations living in and around his Hudson's Bay Company trading post. As the Fort's influence waned, some of these teachers, like Richard and Ann Covington, set up their own schools. The log cabin where the Covingtons lived and labored is now a historic treasure, the oldest school building still standing in Clark County.

Some years later, Vancouver's pioneering Mother Joseph—recognized in 1953 by the American Institute of Architects as the Northwest's first architect—persuaded another early settler, Lowell Hidden, to go into the brick-making business. As a result, Mother Joseph was able to construct the massive, cruciform House of Providence to shelter her convent school and orphanage. The Hidden family prospered, and thanks to Lowell Hidden's descendants, the grand old brick building remains a vital presence in the community.

The story is the same today. Educators working to build better schools can count on help from business, while business leaders seeking to attract and keep employees depend on educators to respond to their needs. The result, according to Steve Burdick, director of Economic Development Services for the City of Vancouver, is a healthy, diversified economy and a high quality of life. "Industries choose to come here because of our very solid educational system," he said.

The Southwest Washington Child Care Consortium is a prime example of education responding to business issues. In the late 1980s, several large, high-tech corporations, along with Vancouver's independent, family-owned newspaper, *The Columbian*, alerted Educational Service District 112 (serving Clark and five smaller neighboring counties) to the growing need for pre-school and after-school programs for working families. The Columbia River Economic Development Council (CREDC) helped with planning and fundraising, and in 1989 the ESD opened three centers. Now the largest community-based child-care consortium in the United States, serving nearly 2,000 children in more than 20 centers, the program received a Ford Foundation Innovations in Government award in 1998.

The ESD itself is part of a legislated network providing practical connections and accountability among school districts statewide. Besides serving schools in its six-county area with more than 200 programs such as special education, fiscal oversight, and grant writing, the ESD fosters partnerships for school support among a variety of local entities.

One such partnership, the Columbia River Education and Workforce Council (CREWC), was organized as a nonprofit agency in 1995 in response to business concerns about the skills of students entering the rapidly expanding local workforce. Existing job training programs were mostly designed to help workers with special needs, such as students with disabilities or unemployed adults. CREWC brings business and education leaders together with the goal of building a mainstream workforce prepared to meet the world-class standards of Clark County's employers.

"The purpose of these partnerships is to help children achieve higher standards," said Sharon McFarland,

Mother Joseph designed and supervised construction of Providence Academy, one of Clark County's first schools. The building was completed in 1873. Photo by Cliff Barbour

Discovery Middle School is a member of the Vancouver School District's Challenge magnet program. Photo provided by ESD 112-Region Schools

CREWC's executive director. "We know people learn more and retain more when they can see the relevance of their academic studies in the context of the real world. This is about opening options, not limiting them. It's about giving students plenty of information so they can make better choices for their lives."

To help students act on these choices, school districts in Clark County are teaming with staff at Clark College, one of the state's oldest community colleges and currently the second-largest in a single location. Another key participant is the Washington State University branch campus in Vancouver, an upper division and graduate level institution offering Bachelor's, Master's, and advanced certificate programs. These groundbreaking collaborations have made it possible for career-focused students to condense four years of post-secondary professional training to three, first by earning college credit at Clark on a fast track before and after high school graduation, then by completing a bachelor's degree in two years at WSU. "This is a very effective use of resources for taxpayers," said Dr. Tana Hasart, Clark College president. "It's an extremely efficient way for students to meet their goals, and the community gains a better-qualified workforce in a shorter period of time."

The community in turn supports the schools in countless ways at every academic level. Local businesses provide millions of dollars' worth of equipment, supplies, hands-on learning materials, and staff development opportunities to Vancouver and Clark County schools every year. And dedicated employees work directly with students and families—mentoring, tutoring, and volunteering for special events such as science workshops and culture fairs. Church congregations and faith leaders help with these and many other tasks, as do service organizations, civic groups, and thousands of individual partners who realize the importance of involvement in local education.

Individual school foundations and parent-teacher organizations translate all this energy into tangible results. When one downtown elementary school was due for remodeling, its foundation raised funds to build a swimming pool, with inspiration and substantial financial support from private investor Paul Christensen. The foundation also funds a volunteer coordinator; as a result, the school tallies over 1,000 volunteer hours a month.

Other schools and programs in the county's nine public school districts have equally gratifying stories to tell—stories of success, commitment, overcoming adversity, meeting challenges, and above all, working together. Dr. James Parsley, superintendent of the Vancouver School District (one of the two largest at about 22,000 students), summed it up: "Vision means empowering significant numbers of people to achieve a common goal. It can't just remain an idea on paper, and the people have to be part of it from beginning to end."

Ray Yoder, now in his 12th year as superintendent of Green Mountain School District in the far north county, knows the value of teamwork. If the families, friends, and neighbors of his 126 students weren't working together every day with teachers and staff, their 70-year-old school wouldn't be the lively place it is.

"To get here, I tell people it's north on Pup Crick just below Badger Hollow," said Yoder. "We have no licensed businesses in our

Alki Middle School is one of 33 educational facilities in the Vancouver School District. Photo by Cliff Barbour

area, no stores, taverns, gas stations, only a couple of churches. The school becomes the identity of the community. In some ways you're walking into the 1800s when you come to our school, yet when you go inside, you see the technology, the resources, and you realize you're also preparing for the new millennium."

In other words, Green Mountain knows it isn't alone. "The ESD services are like oxygen," said Yoder. "Without our neighbors at ESD, we probably wouldn't *be*." He also depends on the county's network of superintendents and other educators. "I really appreciate Jim Parsley," he said. "He's so open to dialogue and working with me on issues. The mission of the largest district is really the same as the mission of the smallest—to educate kids in a warm, safe environment and prepare them for life."

This inter-district collaboration takes many forms. The Clark County Skills Center, based in the large east-county Evergreen District but co-owned by eight local districts, has been providing top-quality technical career training for high school students since 1983. The Center for Agriculture, Science and Environmental Education (known as CASEE), on 80 acres in the north-county Battle Ground District, also serves students county-wide in an innovative and highly successful partnership with numerous public agencies and local businesses. Vancouver's model magnet schools in science, the arts, pre-med, pre-law, and other fields are open by application to students throughout the area.

(above) Students in Clark County's public schools benefit from the involvement of families, friends, and businesses throughout their communities. Photo provided by ESD 112-Region Schools

(below) Skyview High School is Vancouver School District's newest high school. It houses the district's science, math, and technology magnet program.

(above and right) The scenic campus of Clark College is home to events that serve the entire area, including cultural activities and community forums. Photos by Cliff Barbour

Washington School for the Deaf and Washington State School for the Blind, both in Vancouver, are an important part of the region's educational network. So are its many excellent private schools, both religious and secular, and other public and private programs for professional training and personal enrichment. Supporting all these is the Fort Vancouver Regional Library System, with branches throughout Clark County and beyond, and inter-library arrangements with a host of other public or specialized libraries, including those at Clark College and WSUV.

In 1989 Dr. Harold Dengerink arrived at the nexus of these community partnerships as executive officer of WSU's new branch campus. He was soon active on several crucial boards linking education, business, economic development, historic preservation, health care, and media—all, in his view, part of the process of reclaiming and building a distinct community identity. "We've had to learn who we are and how we relate together," he said. "We've had to learn what we're proud of."

This is what young people do, too, as they grow to find their place in the world. Vancouver and Clark County couldn't be in a better position to help them do it.

A Portrait of Prosperity

A Portrait of Prosperity

A Foundation For Growth

Chapter 3

We are now in Vancouver, the New York of the Pacific Ocean.

—Narcissa Whitman, missionary, 1836

In Vancouver and throughout Clark County, progress involves both growth and preservation of valuable resources. Photos by Cliff Barbour

(above) Marshall House, built in 1886, is among many refurbished structures on Officers Row. Photo by Cliff Barbour

In September of 1870, General William Tecumseh Sherman, Civil War hero and general-in-chief of the United States Army, visited the Vancouver base to see for himself why there was talk of selling the officers' houses and barracks and opening the land to settlers.

True, some of the buildings were run-down, and regional Army headquarters had moved away—but soldiers and townsfolk feared that without the base, the town would lose its reason for being. They clung to the hope that Sherman's commander-in-chief, President Ulysses S. Grant, who had served here as a young officer, might influence the decision. They tried hard to impress their exalted guest.

Apparently, they succeeded. Reporting on the visit, General E.R.S. Canby, commander of the Army's Department of the Columbia, called this the best place on the Northwest coast to house troops. General Sherman returned often and fondly, paying one last call as commander of the Army in 1883. By that time, he had made sure that Vancouver Barracks would be upgraded to the tune of $50,000 and permanently maintained.

A century later, history repeated itself. The splendid old houses on Officers Row, many raised in the building spree that followed General Sherman's visit, were in decline. Two of them, Grant House (named for the president, though he never lived there) and Marshall House (named for General George C. Marshall, who was headquartered there in the late 1930s as commander of the Fifth Brigade), belonged to local organizations. The city made these structures the centerpiece of its 1978 Central Park plan and subsequently acquired them by trade.

Popular support was intense for acquiring the other buildings as well. The federal government still owned them; Army headquarters had moved north to Fort Lewis 30 years before, but Vancouver remained a training base, and the VA hospital housed its staff on Officers Row. However, in 1981 the government declared the Row houses surplus and moved to sell them one by one on the open market. Local citizens besieged the White House and the GSA state office, backed by Senator Slade Gorton, and in 1984 the houses were deeded to the City of Vancouver.

Once the city owned them, it had to figure out what to do with them. The best alternative appeared to be a mix of residential and commercial uses, but deed restrictions discouraged private financing. "Officers Row was an extremely challenging project—financially daunting and a huge political gamble," said Vancouver economic development services director Steve Burdick.

Potential revenues could not match the cost of restoring the buildings. The city's solution, a complex plan for achieving the $10-million project with tax-exempt bonds, has become a nationwide public financing model, with no shortage of tenants who love being part of living history. As the bonds are retired in the next few years, rents will support parks and other historic projects. "To have it be a commercial success without the necessity of general fund subsidy is a remarkable feat," Burdick said. "If you scale that kind of mountain, you feel you can do it again."

Even before Officers Row was completed in 1988, Vancouver had begun to envision its Columbia River Renaissance—if anything, a more daunting project, much larger in scope, with many more public and private partners. The Renaissance plan was unveiled in October 1992, along with a memorial to Captain Vancouver, thus marking the 200th anniversary of his lieutenant's first exploration.

The plan presents the Renaissance vision in five separate statements: urban design and public access, economic development, environmental stewardship, historic resources, and recreation. "The fact that we couched the same idea in five different plans, from five different points of view, was the unique reason it was recognized as one of the best urban plans in the nation," said Kelly Punteney, a Vancouver parks planner whose passion for reclaiming the city shoreline for the widest possible use has driven the Renaissance idea from the start.

Renaissance elements include a series of parks, restaurants, condos and townhouses, business and industrial parks, shipyards and boat basins, preserved wetlands, the city's innovative Water Resources Education Center, and a public walkway linking them all together. The most recent trail link, north through downtown and west along the Mill Plain Boulevard Extension, connects these new upstream developments with Vancouver Lake and Frenchman's Bar recreational areas far downstream.

The Mill Plain Extension itself was a spectacular exercise in partnership, many years in the planning. It eventually involved nine major backers, including the Port of Vancouver. The roadway serves as a major new arterial that streamlines access from interstate highways to west-side industrial lands across the downtown core. The

(above) By the 1920s, cars were beginning to replace horses at Vancouver Barracks. Photo courtesy of Vancouver National Historic Reserve Trust

(below) Vancouver Barracks, established in 1849, served as the military headquarters for much of the Pacific Northwest. Photo by Cliff Barbour

number of jobs available through the Port has tripled since the project has allowed access to hundreds of additional acres of industrial land.

The city's current focus is on downtown development, centered around Esther Short Park—a special events and convention center to the south, sparkling new mixed-use residential and commercial buildings to the east and north, and walkways connecting the park with the National Historic Reserve and Officers Row. As these projects take shape around it, the park is being restored, with a new public plaza designed to become the community's living room.

"The key to revitalizing a city is having people who live there," said downtown developer Elie Kassab, a relative newcomer to Vancouver who saw downtown Portland through a similar revival as a founding member of the Association for Portland Progress. "When that happens, the services these people use will flourish."

Luepke Florist, a Vancouver fixture, has been in Dianne Frichtl's family for three generations. "I'm quite excited about what I see now," she said. "The timing is right, with a combination of private investment, enabling tax laws, and political will. The waterfront is the beginning of the rest of the positive development downtown. It's becoming a river community again."

(above) Camas Meadows Golf Club, an upscale 18-hole public course, opened in summer 2000. The scenic, par-72 course contains more than 40 acres of wetlands.

(below) Recent renovations have made Esther Short Park a focal point of downtown revitalization. Photos by Cliff Barbour

In 1990 legislative passage of a state Growth Management Plan set the stage for local plans in the unincorporated county and its cities and towns. Clark County business leaders established the Responsible Growth Forum to create consensus on tough issues and recommend positive long-term solutions. At about the same time, the Greater Vancouver Chamber of Commerce helped launch Identity Clark County, providing a way for corporate leadership and investment to support economic expansion and vitality throughout the wider community.

"Growth" and "management" can be fighting words. The process has not been without conflict, as development swallows 2,000 acres of farmland each year and a modern urban economy overrides a rural way of life. That life produced many robust small communities, each of which now faces its own version of the challenge confronting the county as a whole—namely, sustaining community strength and identity in the face of change.

"We provide a wide variety of public forums to give longtime residents and newcomers an opportunity to engage in dialogue," said Bill Fromhold, past president of the Greater Vancouver Chamber of Commerce. "Even when we disagree on aspects of public policy, everyone has the same goal in mind; a vibrant, livable community with a strong business climate that's also good for families, schools, neighborhoods. The pathways may be different, but the good news is that we share a positive goal."

Sharp Corporation, in the east county town of Camas, is just one of many companies that have entered wholeheartedly into this dialogue. Drawn to the area in the late 1980s by the business-friendly environment, high quality of life, outstanding educational resources, and close proximity to Portland International Airport and other regional amenities, the microelectronics firm has chosen to stay in spite of changes in its own corporate structure.

"That's the kind of thing that happens," said Tony Bacon, a public relations consultant, publisher, and longtime local observer. "We're attracting and keeping companies that could have relocated. Sharp is Japanese-owned, but it isn't in Japan—it's in Camas, because they like it there."

Esther Short Park's new playground features a family atmosphere. Photo by Cliff Barbour

(left) Sightseers can view the Columbia River from a three-story lookout at the Henry J. Kaiser Shipyard Memorial and Interpretive Center. The memorial pays tribute to shipbuilder Henry J. Kaiser and the workers who built 141 vessels during World War II.

(opposite) The Vancouver Farmers Market, open from April through October, sparks residents' growing delight in their refurbished downtown.

(below) A gazebo on the old parade grounds across from Officers Row invites visitors to rest and relax. Photos by Cliff Barbour

A Portrait of Prosperity

A Portrait of Prosperity

A Spirit of Unity

Chapter 4

The good old chief here took his leave of the party. In commemoration of his friendly behaviour, and his residence being in the neighborhood, this part of the river obtained the name of FRIENDLY REACH.

—from the journals of Capt. George Vancouver, reporting on Lt. Broughton's explorations of the Columbia River, November, 1792

In Clark County, neighbors share bonds of friendship and close ties to their communities. Photos by Cliff Barbour

Lieutenant William Broughton didn't know what to expect when he crossed the Columbia bar in late autumn of 1792 in the brig Chatham. No other river on the whole Pacific coast offered entry into the continental heartland. Would this be the exception? Would it in fact prove to be the long-dreamed-of Northwest Passage to rivers flowing toward the Atlantic? Captain Vancouver had sent the lieutenant to find out.

The oldest apple tree in the Northwest grows at Old Apple Tree Park, located on Columbia Way. The tree was planted in 1826. Photo by Cliff Barbour

Anchoring in the estuary and taking two smaller boats upstream, Broughton met several canoes full of natives. An old village headman became his guide as far as the rock-walled gorge of the wild river and interceded on his behalf with suspicious warriors along the way. At mile 128, Broughton turned back, declining the old chief's invitation to visit his home village at mile 110, across from Point Vancouver, but calling that part of the river "the Friendly Reach"— a name found on charts even today.

The old chief's people had lived along the river for 3,000 to 4,000 years in rectangular cedar plank houses that could be taken apart and moved from place to place. One such house was continuously occupied for four centuries. The people flourished on the river's abundance, fishing from large seaworthy cedar canoes with seine nets. They were not a tribe, but rather a family-centered society of diverse groups connected by language and custom, and known to European explorers as the Chinook. They were long-practiced traders when the newcomers found them, and the language that arose from this encounter—the Chinook Jargon, or Oregon Trade Language—formed a bridge between two worlds.

More than anywhere else, these worlds converged on the north shore of the Friendly Reach. The trading post called Fort Vancouver officially opened when Hudson's Bay Company western governor Sir George Simpson smashed a bottle of rum on the flagstaff in March 1825. But the site was more than simply headquarters for Simpson's domain. It was a crossroads for traffic from all parts of the globe— French Canadian voyageurs and their Iroquois guides, Chinook entrepreneurs, English, Scottish, and Irish traders and trappers and journeymen of all kinds, Yankee merchants and missionaries, Orkney Islanders from the Scottish coast, Kanakas from the Sandwich Islands, people of tribes far and wide—all presided over by the Big Doctor, the White-Headed Eagle, John McLoughlin himself.

In his hands the post thrived. Seeking to hold the land above the river for the British, he urged homesteaders to move south, but partly because of his own good husbandry, the tide of settlement overwhelmed him. He himself moved south in 1846, the year the present Canadian border was established at the 49th parallel. Oregon Territory came into being two years later, and the Hudson's Bay Company withdrew to Victoria, Canada. On May 13, 1849, Major John Hatheway's troops arrived on the U.S.S. *Massachusetts* and set up camp, forming the new lodestone for the neighborhood that was already here.

Ties to that neighborhood, the first of its kind in the Northwest, remain strong today. Vancouver's pocket-sized Old Apple Tree Park protects a lone survivor from Dr. McLoughlin's bounteous orchards. A reconstructed Fort Vancouver receives thousands of visitors each year, and Christmas celebrations on the fort site have continued annually since Dr. McLoughlin hosted the first one. People

whose grandparents helped build Officers Row now labor alongside their grandchildren to preserve it.

Even the geography of Vancouver reflects its past. The natural prairies behind the Army base that the soldiers called plains are retained today as major east-west arterials, Mill Plain and Fourth Plain boulevards. The watershed and greenbelt traversing the city, now known as Burnt Bridge Creek, used to be simply Bridge Creek before a fire destroyed the original Fourth Plain crossing. The names of neighborhoods—Harney Heights (the state's oldest), Fisher's Landing, Fruit Valley, Hudson's Bay, North Garrison, and many more—tell the region's story. Like children whose lives expand and connect as they mature, each neighborhood brings its own distinct character to the community as a whole.

In 1992, nearly a century after her great-great-uncle served at Vancouver Barracks with one of the renowned black U.S. Cavalry units called Buffalo Soldiers, Leann Johnson helped launch the YWCA's Diversity Task Force, which she directed for eight years. Together with city and county staff, elected officials, community leaders, and neighborhood associations, the Task Force seeks to strengthen Vancouver's formative tradition of diversity through education, awareness, and policy.

The Vancouver Housing Authority's enforcement of the federal Fair Housing Act after World War II made that job easier, according to one of the region's premier historians, Pat Jollota, a member of Vancouver's city council. "People of all races were sold homes

At the Fort Vancouver Historic Site, cultural demonstrations and guided tours provide a look at the lives of Clark County's early settlers. Photos by Cliff Barbour

anywhere," she wrote. "The end result is that today we have no ethnic neighborhoods in Clark County—no ghetto, no barrio, no Chinatown. We escaped much of the turmoil that would sweep other cities because of the actions of the VHA then."

We also lack the cultural density that such neighborhoods can provide. Instead of being concentrated together, ethnic threads from across the world are scattered throughout our social fabric. Our history is our collective culture, and we're young enough to feel connected with it in very personal ways, and seasoned enough to know the value of carrying it forward. "This is the richest community on the Pacific coast in history and heritage," said Vernon Stoner, Vancouver city manager from 1996 to 2000. "By making the most of our assets, we have an opportunity to educate the entire region."

As Clark County's population escalates, so does the perennial challenge of bringing newcomers into the community—weaving them into the fabric, helping them realize what was here when they arrived and what they can add to it. In the process, many longtime residents are discovering the richness of their own home ground. This is the work of the county's Neighborhood Outreach program and the City of Vancouver's Office of Neighborhood Services.

Neighborhood associations have been officially recognized in Vancouver since 1976. As governments began more actively cultivating neighborhood partnerships, the number of associations in the city alone ballooned to a total of over 50 by late 1999, with many more in the county and smaller communities. In 1995 Vancouver was honored as a NUSA Notable by Neighborhoods USA. Two years later the neighborhood program received an award from the National League of Cities for its work with young people.

Vancouver provides a nationwide model for involving citizens in public decision-making on everything from spring cleaning and block parties to transportation and growth issues. "Our unusual level of neighborhood involvement in new development builds good working partnerships between residents and developers," said Grace Farmer, Neighborhood Services coordinator. "We're also a liaison between residents and city staff. This helps employees realize who they work for and become more passionate about their jobs and responsibilities."

But it's the people who make the neighborhood networks go. Government offices just supply the infrastructure. As word gets around on Clark County's relatively low housing costs, excellent schools, economic stability, and links to a major urban center—all in a state with no income tax—neighbors here realize that the strength of their communities cannot be left to chance. They know it's up to them to make sure that their neighborhood is more than just an address. Thanks to their proud investment in the place where they live, the Friendly Reach continues to live up to its name. ❦

(above) Esther Short Park has been a gathering spot in Vancouver since 1855.

(opposite) New homes are bringing residents back to Vancouver's riverfront area. Photos by Cliff Barbour

Leaders in Vancouver and Clark County are dedicated to preserving a family-friendly environment. Photos by Cliff Barbour

A Portrait of Prosperity

A Portrait of Prosperity

A Community that Cares

Chapter 5

Field and forest, not buildings and blacktop,

provide the livability we all cherish.

—Tom Koenninger, editor and vice president,
The Columbian, December 19, 1999

(left) Clark County residents continue a tradition of environmental stewardship. Photos by Cliff Barbour

When Battle Ground teacher Tim Hicks first dreamed in 1985 of an agricultural school for all Clark County students, he was aware that the Patrick Hough Estate already funded agriculture education in his district. What he didn't yet know was how precisely that very dream had been spelled out in a will written 70 years before.

(above) Providence Academy, constructed in the 1870s, remains a vital presence in Vancouver. Photo by Cliff Barbour

Born in 1846 by the River Shannon in Slevoire, County Tipperary, Ireland, the young schoolmaster Paddy Hough lost his left arm in the Franco-Prussian War, along with his illusions about the quarrels of kings. He made his way to the New World and eventually to Vancouver, where he directed the Academy at St. James Cathedral and later became a legendary teacher and principal in city and county public schools. He and his wife, Ann, lived frugally and left a substantial estate "to the purpose of establishing an Agricultural High School" in Clark County.

"I'd never seen the will," Hicks recalled. "For me, the idea developed from a conference I attended. We found a site and started signing on partners, and our dream of an integrated curriculum with relevant hands-on activities began to come true."

The Center for Agriculture, Science, and Environmental Education prospered on its woods and fields, providing a high school "land laboratory" and community learning center for students of all ages—a model for such programs across the country. Not until CASEE was well established did Hicks actually read Patrick Hough's description of the school he had in mind. Almost to the letter, it was the school that had come to pass, nurtured quietly over the years by its foresighted benefactor.

"Some of the quotes from the will were kind of eerie," Hicks said. "He had dreamed of a curriculum like ours, on a site exactly the size of ours, near an incorporated city. He imagined it just as we came up with it. He wanted it to be called Slevoire Hall, after his birthplace. We might still do that."

A partnership across time, animating an idea that seems meant to be—such stories crop up again and again in the annals of Clark County stewardship. Perhaps the most comprehensive is the Vancouver National Historic Reserve, established by Congress on November 11, 1996, on 366 acres of public land in the heart of the city.

The vision of "one place across time" helped guide this achievement to the security of Reserve status. Management partners are the City of Vancouver, the U.S. Army, the State of Washington, and the National Park Service. The Vancouver National Historic Reserve Trust was created to support the partnership, whose goals for all components of the Reserve are preservation, education/interpretation, and public use and accessibility.

The Park Service operates the Fort Vancouver National Historic Site, including the reconstructed trading post and a museum and visitor center. On nearby Officers Row, the restored homes of General Oliver Otis Howard and General George C. Marshall are also part of the Reserve. So is the original commander's home now named for President Ulysses S. Grant, who served as a quartermaster in the early days of Vancouver Barracks, although he never lived in this house.

The Barracks, too, are part of the Reserve, with the oldest surviving buildings dating back to 1887. After commemorating 150 years of service at the site, the Army has ended its tenure. City officials and the Reserve Trust board, encouraged by the success of the Officers Row restoration, envision the Barracks as a center for historical education mixed with commercial and residential uses.

The Reserve also includes Pearson Field, recognized by the Smithsonian Institution as the oldest working airfield in the country, and the Air Museum in the Murdock Aviation Center. This complex, recognizing the contributions of early aviators, is named for noted Army flyer Lieutenant Alexander Pearson Jr. and Vancouver businessman, pilot, and philanthropist Jack Murdock. In 1937, during General Marshall's command of the Vancouver post, the Soviet transpolar flight of Valeri P. Chkalov landed at Pearson Field. A nearby monument marks this historic event.

The Water Resources Education Center, toward the upstream end of the Renaissance Trail, completes the Historic Reserve, demonstrating in countless ways how a city and its environment can thrive together. Beautiful buildings in a natural river setting house museum exhibits, educational programs, and some of the community's most attractive public meeting spaces. Advanced water and sewage treatment systems, which blend unobtrusively into the Center grounds, have consistently earned state awards for exemplary operation.

Other examples of environmental stewardship abound throughout the county. Habitat Partners unites business, government, nonprofit groups, schools, and property owners to preserve and enhance fish and wildlife habitat and provide environmental education to children. The Columbia Land Trust works with families and communities to conserve signature landscapes and vital habitat all along the river. Legions of volunteers support dozens of organizations with related goals.

Corporate and family donations dating back decades have preserved green spaces, from Vancouver Lake Regional Park in the

Reenactors at the Fort Vancouver Historic Site work year-round to preserve and share Clark County's history. Photos by Cliff Barbour

Visitors can sample rural life in the 1920s at Pomeroy Living History Farm. The farm features a six-bedroom log cabin, vegetable garden, and blacksmith shop. Photos by Cliff Barbour

western lowlands to the East Fork Lewis River Greenway in the north-county community of La Center. Property taxes dedicated to conservation have helped local entities acquire well over 2,000 acres of open lands on most major lakes and stream systems.

Historic preservation, too, is by no means limited to the Vancouver Reserve. The Fort Vancouver Historical Society, founded in 1917, is expanding into new quarters from the Carnegie Library building, its home since the mid-1960s. Similar efforts flourish on a smaller scale in the north-county logging town of Amboy, and in Camas and Washougal to the east, where the logs were milled. Far to the north in the hamlet of Ariel, the late Chief Don Lelooska's family continues a tradition—carefully tending the history and culture of the region's native peoples in their museum and longhouse.

On Cedar Creek west of Amboy, an 1876 grist mill has been restored as a working museum where visitors can grind their own grain flour to take home. At Pomeroy Living History Farm on the Lewis River, year-round events introduce guests to rural life in the 1920s, the delights of herb gardening, and teatime, English style. The railroad past the farm is being rehabilitated by the nonprofit volunteer Battle Ground, Yacolt & Chelatchie Prairie Railway Association, while Battle Ground's Steam Team #539 works to rebuild a 1917 steam engine and bring its music back to the valley.

These and hundreds of other projects are bountifully supported by various local foundations. The Southwest Washington Community

Foundation, launched in 1984, holds endowed funds for 24 local organizations, and manages scores of other funds established by individuals, families, and businesses. One such fund assists the local "I Have A Dream" Foundation in assuring post-secondary education to children who might not otherwise receive it. Vancouver supports more sponsored classes per capita than any other city in this nation-wide program.

Southwest Washington Medical Center at Vancouver, the state's largest nonprofit health-care center south of Puget Sound, serves the community with a Level II Trauma Center, an oncology center, and a breast care center. Other services include the Healthy Steps Women's and Children's Clinic, and the Family Medicine primary care residency training program. The Center's major health-care partners include Vancouver Clinic, Kaiser Permanente, and Northwest Surgical Specialists—physicians for major sports teams in the area, including the Portland Trail Blazers.

Also vital to the strength of Clark County's caring network is its media voice. In continuous publication since 1890, *The Columbian* newspaper serenely avoids discussion of giant media buyouts. "Our role in the community is more important than the big check," said publisher Scott Campbell, whose grandfather bought the paper in 1921. "We intend to continue to be part of the community discussion, both editorially and face to face."

(above) A network of health-care providers offers state-of-the-art care to Clark County residents. Photo courtesy of Kaiser Permanente

(below) Southwest Washington Medical Center serves critically ill and injured patients with a Level II trauma center. Photo by Cliff Barbour

In addition to daily coverage of global, national, and community events, *The Columbian* provides information to the entire metro region from its fast-growing Web site. Venerable smaller papers—*The Reflector* and the *Camas-Washougal Post-Record*—cover the north and east county, while other local news mainstays are CVTV cable, KVAN radio, and the *Vancouver Business Journal*.

At the heart of all of these efforts, of course, are the people who live here. From schoolchildren to millionaires, Clark County is full of generous givers—far too many to name. George and Carolyn Propstra have returned community support of their regional restaurant chain, giving more than $12 million in recent years to athletic, civic, and scholastic projects. The "Northeanders," neighbors in Ridgefield, make a tradition of preparing holiday meals for needy families. Ray Hickey, who in 40 years on the river rose from deckhand to sole owner of Tidewater Barge Lines, donated $1 million worth of waterfront property back to the city for a major link in the Renaissance Trail. And volunteers of all ages at the North County Community Food Bank give their time to help local families build stable, independent, productive lives. The list goes on and on.

John Marshall, a retired Vancouver city administrator and 1999 First Citizen who has devoted many years to realizing the vision of "one place across time" at the Historic Reserve, shrugged off the notion that he invented the phrase. "Everything is borrowed in this world," he said. "But the more you look at this place, the more you realize that you have a unique story, one that will continue to grow across time. It's evolving through the awareness of a lot of people, and it continues to unfold and get richer as we go along."

Marshall was talking about the Reserve—but his words sum up the community that has deemed this and so much more to be worth saving.

(left) Marshall House is among 21 stately Victorian houses on Officers Row. Thanks to the efforts of countless Clark County residents, the once-neglected homes now serve as a showpiece for the city.

(opposite page) Cedar Creek Gristmill is the state's only fully restored 19th century grain-grinding mill. The facility is open to the public for weekend tours. Photos by Cliff Barbour

Visitors are invited to tour the Water Resources Education Center, an environmental showcase that also provides vital water treatment services to the area. Photos by Cliff Barbour

A Portrait of Prosperity

Recreation & Celebrations

Chapter 6

The scenery of this place is sublime. High, well-wooded hills, mountains covered with perpetual snow, extensive natural meadows and plains… covered with a rich sward of grass and a profusion of flowering plants.

—Scottish botanist David Douglas, arriving by canoe at Fort Vancouver in April, 1825

(left) On water and land, Clark County provides many avenues to adventure. A statue of the Chinook noblewoman Illchee overlooks Vancouver's new riverfront development. Photos by Cliff Barbour

(above) People and pets stroll the riverfront during "Walk for the Animals," a fund-raiser to benefit the Southwest Washington Humane Society.

(below) Even in the heart of the city, Vancouver residents can connect with nature. Photos by Cliff Barbour

It took Thomas Jefferson's Corps of Discovery more than two years to travel 8,000 miles from St. Louis to the Pacific and back again. Together, the Vancouver's Discovery Walkers take just one spring weekend to walk several times that far.

Of course, Lewis and Clark had a few more obstacles to contend with, and the weather was a lot worse. Late April in Vancouver can be heaven, with drifts of angel hair across crystal skies, mild maritime breezes, flowering cherry and plum and rhododendron on a backdrop of sparkling green—perfect for walking. Even the rains in April are misty green, reminding us why this place remains so beautifully alive in all seasons.

Thanks to an established walking culture in Vancouver and a well-developed urban trail system, the International Marching League chose this city to host the nation's only IML-sanctioned annual walk. More than 1,000 people from 15 nations gathered to help Vancouver celebrate its third Discovery Walk Festival in 1999. Most completed several jaunts of 5K to 42K, for a total of 2,500 individual walks in three days.

Tree-lined streets take cyclists on a summer road trip through the city.
Photo by Cliff Barbour

The same year, in its second annual Walkable Community Awards, the July-August issue of *Walking* magazine named Vancouver one of the top 10 walking cities in America. It's easy to see why after a stroll along the river, or past the parade grounds and back up through the Barracks, or out Lower River Road to Vancouver Lake. Planners, donors, and volunteers have worked hard to make it easy. Before they're done, a tracery of walking trails will branch out to the farthest corners of the county.

A walker-friendly environment connects people with nature, life, and each other in more ways than one. Seeing the world from a human height, at a human pace, helps us appreciate all it has to offer. Vancouver and Clark County provide dozens of opportunities to do just that—including orienteering around Battle Ground Lake, Saturday Academy science classes for youngsters at the Water Resources Education Center, and rambles through the region's greenways, parks, and refuges.

Walkers at the Ridgefield National Wildlife Refuge, for instance, can monitor the migration of cranes, swans, and geese on the Pacific Flyway. From the Refuge south past Vancouver Lake to the river shore, many more species of birds and other wildlife can be seen feeding in the diverse landscape of wooded brush and rich bottomland.

Several popular downtown walking routes, including the River Renaissance Trail, also accommodate runners, cyclists, and in-line skaters. Along the way, adventurers can browse retail shops and galleries, the Vancouver Farmers Market, and the Grant House Folk Art Center, or step back in time at the Pearson Air Museum and

The International Festival highlights the area's cultural diversity with a day of ethnic music, dance, and food. Photos by Cliff Barbour

Dr. McLoughlin's herb garden. These places are accessible by car, of course, but there's a joy in arriving under one's own power that's particularly suited to Vancouver.

Walking with a purpose extends to the county's well-tended golf courses, including several executive par-3 layouts and a challenging all-day course that has hosted national tournament play. Clark County hosts other national contests, too, when boat crews bring their racing shells to Vancouver Lake, and baseball teams convene at the multimillion-dollar Propstra Field in the city's Central Park.

Vancouver also offers two indoor sports arenas with full-sized soccer fields and professional turf, a six-court basketball facility, a tennis and racquetball center, three indoor public pools downtown, and the only indoor ice arena in the Northwest that has two NHL-sized rinks—the practice home of the Western Hockey League's Portland Winter Hawks. A new YMCA has two more pools and a rock-climbing wall.

Back outdoors, serious athletes find hiking, rock-climbing, and backpacking challenges in the Gifford Pinchot National Forest and the Silver Star Range at the county's eastern border, and fabulous

The Columbia River is a worldwide mecca for sailboarders.
Photo by Cliff Barbour

downhill and cross-country skiing an hour or two from downtown. The East Fork of the Lewis is not only a premium steelhead trout stream, but also one of the region's most cherished whitewater rivers for kayaking, canoeing, and rafting. Sailboarders skim the Columbia like butterflies, while sailboats cluster by the hundreds near the Interstate Bridge on cloudless summer days.

It figures that a "walking town" would love a parade. Vancouver's Veterans Day Parade is the largest west of the Mississippi, with over 3,000 marchers through downtown and the old Reserve. The Hazel Dell Parade of Bands boasts "Seventy-Six Trombones" and then some. And Battle Ground's Rose Float, the only Portland Rose Festival Parade entry still built exclusively by volunteers, encores in the hometown Harvest Days Parade a few weeks after its annual June appearance on national television.

Fort Vancouver has its own celebration, and so do other towns around the county. Camas Days and La Center's Our Day reflect the history and character of those communities. Ridgefield has its Pioneer Days, complete with strawberry shortcake and fireworks. In Amboy, visitors can savor logging contests and baked salmon at Territorial Days and Native American tribal arts at the Tum Tum Encampment.

St. Joseph's Sausage Festival is a Vancouver tradition, supporting the parish school by serving its renowned sausage menu every autumn to crowds who've been waiting all year. The Wine & Jazz Festival draws thousands downtown in late September, benefiting local nonprofits with a mix of great food and Northwest wines, art, and music.

Clark County's festivals whet the appetite for its restaurants—from international fare to the trendiest Northwest cuisine. And the region's restaurateurs are among its most generous citizens. George Propstra continues to set the standard with proceeds from his landmark Holland Restaurant and his Burgerville chain. People who swarm to Beaches for the food and the river ambiance help owner/partner Mark Matthias raise over $20,000 a year for local families in need, while NBA hero Kermit Washington's Le Slam Sports Bar supports his passion for improving medical care in Africa.

The year-round feast of art and music that feeds this community's soul has gained international recognition. The works of area sculptors, painters, photographers, and textile and glass artists are prized around the world. Tears of Joy Puppet Theatre has earned global acclaim as well. The Camas concert series hosts the likes of famed choreographer Paul Taylor. The Bravo! series has its own orchestra and chorale, while the Clark College Orchestra and Vancouver Symphony Orchestra sustain world-class soloists and conductors. And when Garrison Keillor assumes on National Public Radio that his guest, acoustic blues guitarist and composer Kelly Joe Phelps, hails from that "newer Vancouver" farther north, Phelps graciously lets it pass.

All of this festivity reaches its zenith in two outstanding and unique events—Vancouver's Fourth of July celebration and the Clark

County Fair. Our riverborne fireworks display is the biggest aerial show in the western United States and among the top five in the nation, while the state's oldest and largest county fair hit the 130-year mark in 1998 with a record attendance of 300,219.

But the magic of these gatherings is not about numbers. People dedicate years of their lives to staging the Fourth of July and the county fair in order to carry the community's history into the future. As the fair's Executive Director Tom Musser put it, "We've strived over the years to be true to our roots, but also to present what's new. That's what fairs do. The good memories are here, but we try to create new memories."

Folks come to the 10-day Clark County Fair for an endless variety of agricultural and commercial exhibits and top-notch entertainment—to say nothing of the Dairy Women's real ice cream milkshakes, the fresh-picked corn on the cob, the pancake breakfasts, elephant ears, cotton candy, and carnival rides. Florence Robison has been helping 4-H kids get ready for the fair and judging and supervising exhibits since the 1940s. "It was something people looked forward to," she said. "They worked the farm the year 'round, and they were happy to display the fruits of their labors, just like now. Also, they wanted to show what can be done when groups work together."

For the same reasons, Jim Larson has been with the Fourth of July Committee almost since it set off its first rocket. "It's a unique blend of organizations working together," said Larson, a retired fire commissioner who is now the committee's executive director. "There's a satisfaction to being any little piece of this thing that so many people enjoy. It could very easily go away and never happen again. The thought of that gets my stubborn streak going."

The celebration began in 1962, when the Elks Lodge decided to give the city an old-fashioned family day of picnicking and games in the park, ending with fireworks. Larson remembers when the planning used to start around mid-May. Now he labors all year, with a $300,000 budget and masses of volunteers, so 60,000 people can spend the day at the Reserve and settle on blankets at dusk to see the sky explode.

Thousands watch from the water and the surrounding hills, and an estimated 2.5 million more catch the show on TV. But remote access can't match the feeling of sitting on the grass in the dark in a great crowd, oohing and aahing with one voice as the stars burst overhead. And afterward, walking back to your car (or back home, if you're lucky), draped in blankets and sleepy children, you know you've made memories that could only happen here.

Each August, visitors to the Clark County Fair find thrilling rides, top entertainment, thousands of exhibits, and plenty of food. The 10-day event attracts more than 250,000 people every year. Photos by Cliff Barbour

A Portrait of Prosperity

The Clark County Fair is fun for all kinds of kids. Photo by Cliff Barbour

(right) Vintage cars take over the streets of downtown Vancouver during summer's Uptown Village Festival Cruise-In.

(below) Vancouver's 40 et 8 Locomotive draws cheers during the Veterans Day Parade. The locomotive is owned by Voiture Local No. 99 and is used for the Legionnaire group's many fund-raising activities. Photos by Cliff Barbour

Sailors on Vancouver Lake drift away on a lazy summer day.
Photo by Cliff Barbour

A Portrait of Prosperity

A Regional Identity

Chapter 7

The river doesn't separate us. It connects us.

—Mayor Royce Pollard, at an Arbor Day tree-planting by Portland schoolchildren at Vancouver's Marine Park, April 14, 1996

(left) Bonneville Lock and Dam, 40 miles upstream from Vancouver on the Columbia, provides power to the entire Northwest. Photos by Cliff Barbour

In the painting, it is night. The snowy mountain towers above green banks and a dark river. Flame gushes from its wounded flank and billows into a black cloud. Men sit or stand in two dugout canoes, gazing and pointing. The orange light glows back at the volcano from their naked bodies, the calm water, the trees in full leaf.

(above) On Mount St. Helens, scientists at the National Volcanic Monument study the effects of the volcano's 1980 eruption. Photo by Cliff Barbour

This is how artist Paul Kane imagined the eruption of Mount St. Helens, although he never actually saw it. Lodging at Fort Vancouver in December 1846, after a harrowing late-autumn trek across the Rockies with a party of trappers, he listened to witnesses describe the cataclysm of five years before. The volcano's eruptive phase had not yet ended. He thought he might get lucky.

When the weather broke in March, he put a canoe into the swollen Columbia and set off around the bend with two native guides. Passing the mouth of the Lewis on a clear day, he stopped to sketch the massive, distant cone—and just then, as if to mock him, it gave off a stream of white smoke that settled over the summit like a cap on a mushroom.

Paul Kane's visions, actual or imagined, do not match the reality that we in Clark County experienced on May 18, 1980. Scientists and loggers had reported for weeks that the mountain was waking up, but to us it looked as pristine as ever—until the bright spring morning when it came apart. We raced outside and watched an enormous billowing dark-gray mass rise from the mountain, but we saw no fire.

Meanwhile, to the east, the sky went dark, and people thought the world was ending. A magnitude 5+ earthquake had fractured the volcano's north face, and a vast exhalation of ash, rock, and hot gases exploded northward across the timbered wilderness at 120 miles per hour, killing everything in its path. What we saw rising above the familiar south face was the former top 1,200 feet of Mount St. Helens—now a plume of pulverized rock 11 miles high.

We will never stop learning from Mount St. Helens. One of its greatest lessons has to do with the arbitrariness of manmade borders. The eruption refocused our towns and cities, revealing this land as nature made it. Clark County and Portland residents, chance beneficiaries of geology, could only imagine the outcome had it been the south face that exploded. As we worked together to dig ash and mud from rivers and restore services to stalled communities, we gained a sense of regional identity that continues to blossom.

We know now that it is more than just Mount St. Helens that makes us one region. It is also the great Columbia River—not a barrier between us, but a treasure we share. It is Mount Hood, Mount Adams, Mount Rainier, and indeed the entire range of snowy mountains we call the Cascades, intersected by the spectacular Columbia River Gorge. It is the Pacific coast, the ocean beyond, and all that lives in it and because of it. These are our common bonds.

Recognizing these bonds, people throughout the region are collaborating to strengthen them. Alliances among Vancouver and Clark County agencies and advocacy groups are expanding into wider associations across traditional borderlines. As they seek ways to cooperate so that private interests are respected and mutual interests are preserved, stakeholders on all sides are taking their cue from

(above) Children learn about daily life in another era at Fort Vancouver.

(below) Mount Hood, in the Cascade Mountain range, is a favorite spot for campers, hikers, and climbers. Photos by Cliff Barbour

nature. Whether the subject is salmon recovery or habitat restoration or air quality, at some point someone is likely to note that fish and birds and clear days know no boundaries.

For example, the locally controlled Southwest Clean Air Agency deals with air pollution in five southwest Washington counties, and coordinates planning with the Oregon Department of Environmental Quality. SW Clean Air also works with the Washington Department of Ecology and the Southwest Washington Health District.

The two states "didn't necessarily talk to each other 20 years ago," said Bob Elliott, the agency's executive director since 1992. "We had different views, and we went about our business accordingly. We've turned that around completely in the last few years. With roughly 50,000 vehicles commuting daily from Clark County to work in Portland, and 10,000 more commuting the other way, we've realized we have to partner in order to be successful."

Transportation-related matters are foremost on everyone's agenda as Clark County continues to bring the lion's share of population growth into the region. Counties in each state have worked together

Sightseers will find several levels of tumbling waterfalls along the Lewis River. Photo by Cliff Barbour

for years to address common concerns. Now these bodies have formed a Bi-State Transportation Committee to gain a broader view of the problems and develop region-wide strategies for addressing them. Business leaders from both states are taking an active role in the dialogue.

To be sure, the growing prevalence of such discussions does not make them painless. There are no isolated issues, no easy answers. Proposals to dredge the Columbia channel to accommodate deep-draft vessels, for instance, threaten plans for salmon recovery, while proposals to save salmon runs by breaching hydroelectric dams threaten the availability of clean, low-cost public power and river transportation. The difference now is that instead of reacting with fear and hostility, people representing various points of view are becoming ever more willing to sit down together and work out solutions.

Our evolving gift for cooperation has not escaped national notice. In "The 50 Most Alive Places to Live" (*Modern Maturity*, May-June, 2000), Portland and Vancouver share sixth place in the "Green & Clean" category. Successful partnerships like the two-state, four-county Metropolitan Greenspaces Program help attract attention to what the article called our shared "outdoor playgrounds" and Vancouver's "strong sense of community."

Vancouver Mayor Royce Pollard and Portland Mayor Vera Katz foster a working relationship on matters affecting both cities. The Greater Vancouver Chamber of Commerce is reaching out productively not only to the Portland Chamber, but also to smaller Chambers around Clark County. As the region takes charge of its destiny by strengthening local ties, it becomes a stronger and more visible player in the wider national and international community.

Perhaps no collaboration illustrates this better than the array of educational programs, events, and activities known as Celebrate Freedom, sponsored by the Vancouver National Historic Reserve Trust. Highlighting these events is the annual George C. Marshall Lecture Series, which has welcomed such luminaries as Secretary of State Madeleine Albright and General Colin L. Powell.

The General George C. Marshall Public Service Leadership Award annually honors a Clark County resident for leadership ability and commitment to public service. Other Celebrate Freedom events include the city's Veterans Day Parade and a USO-style dance at Pearson Air Museum. Most recently, the Fourth of July gathering has joined the Celebrate Freedom program, along with a sponsors' dinner, "Star Spangled Gala," to help raise funds.

Each year, the George C. Marshall Lecturer's visit to Vancouver includes a trip to Marshall Elementary School, also named for Vancouver's most illustrious citizen. The lecture series is held at Hudson's Bay High School, with the goal of preserving for future generations General Marshall's legacy of courage and leadership.

In June 2000, the series was privileged to welcome NBC news anchor Tom Brokaw, along with more than half of the individuals profiled in his book, *The Greatest Generation*—"ordinary people," he wrote, "whose lives are laced with the markings of greatness." At the same time, many of their local and regional contemporaries were honored in a ceremony on the parade grounds of the Reserve. The occasion offered a unique opportunity for Celebrate Freedom to pay tribute to citizens of the world in an appropriate setting, fulfilling its mission to "help define the City of Vancouver and the Vancouver National Historic Reserve in relation to its past and its future."

Events like these give the people of Vancouver and Clark County a unique perspective on our home turf, providing us with both intimacy and distance. Thanks to the visionaries who keep our history alive, our sense of kinship with other inhabitants of this place spans boundaries of time and terrain.

We sense their presence at the site of the 1,500-year-old Chinookan village of Cathlapotle on the Ridgefield Refuge, near where Paul Kane paused to sketch Mount St. Helens, and at the gristmill on Cedar Creek, and in the galleries of Officers Row. Their homes and workplaces are not off-limits to us, but living strongholds for our own daily achievement. They help us understand ourselves as part of this place, this moment, and also part of something much larger.

Living here, we can share a triumphant musical odyssey with James DePreist and the Oregon Symphony, and the thrill of an NBA

(above) Children experience Native American culture at Fort Vancouver National Historic Site.

(opposite and following page) Clark County residents work to preserve and protect the region's natural beauty. Photos by Cliff Barbour

championship with the Portland Trail Blazers. We can view exhibits like the incomparable Stroganoff family art collection, which made its first U.S. stop at the Portland Art Museum before going to Fort Worth and Paris, then returning to Russia's Hermitage. An abundance of the world's treasures lies at our doorstep and throughout our neighborhood from Canada to California. It's our good fortune that among these treasures is the place we call home.

Photo by Cliff Barbour

A Portrait of Prosperity

Photo by Cliff Barbour

A Portrait of Prosperity

Focus on the Future

Chapter 8

The risks of public investment should not be minimized. But when there is clearly a greater public good, it must be honored as well.

—John White, Chair, Board of Directors, Greater Vancouver Chamber of Commerce, March 2000

(left) Joined by Clark County residents, members of the Nez Perce tribe attend a ceremony honoring their ancestors who were imprisoned at Vancouver Barracks in the 1870s. Photos by Cliff Barbour

We can't fault Meriwether Lewis for underestimating the number of people who would eventually come to the cradle of the great river bend. He was not a prophet, but a soldier and wilderness explorer who liked to go and see, rather than speculate. When he surmised in 1806 that the place could support "40 to 50 thousand souls," he meant it was capable of producing enough corn, beans, and bacon to keep that many people in health. How could he have prophesied strawberries in January? From Mexico?

The Columbia Riverfront Renaissance has reestablished the river's role in daily community life. Photo by Cliff Barbour

When we venture to describe our domain 200 or even 20 years hence, we too, like Lewis, have no idea what unseen forces will affect the outcome. Living as we do on the cusp of one of history's great technological transformations, we can't foretell with certainty what the new era will bring. Unlike Lewis, though, we have some prior knowledge of this place. By tracing the pattern of development up to now, we can begin to imagine how the future might unfold.

People come here now, as they always did, because it's a wonderful place to live. We have plenty of fresh air and clean water, greenspace, streams, trees, mountains. We have big-city attractions, urban amenities, small towns, a viable rural base. We have good roads, traffic that moves, transportation that works. We have business-friendly public policies, relatively low taxes, strong neighborhoods, fine schools, top-quality health care, responsive services, a low crime rate, and a healthy sense of community identity.

This is what people come for. As they keep coming, this is what we must work hard to preserve. Our task is to welcome and adapt to new life while fulfilling our promises to the life that is already here. It is a universal challenge—one that faces any growing family.

Vancouver and Clark County residents are taking it on with gusto.

"We've been talking in the Chamber about the word 'prosperity' and what we as a business organization can do to maintain it," said Steve Dearborn, former vice president of governmental affairs for the Greater Vancouver Chamber of Commerce. "Prosperity is broader than business. It's where people can find diverse job opportunities that enrich their lives in their own neighborhoods and communities. It's where companies can find a climate that nurtures business and provides the quality of life they want for their employees. It's something you can see when you drive down the street. There's a pride, a vitality to it."

Dearborn regards this kind of prosperity as the payoff for years of concerted community effort to adopt and implement a county Growth Management Plan. He sees local developers beginning to partner with residents to create neighborhoods where people can work, shop, and play close to home. Such planned developments strengthen community ties and support families. They also conserve natural resources by reducing dependence on transportation networks.

Businesses do their part by forming nodes around which such neighborhoods can develop. Besides being a magnet for high-tech companies, Clark County still has capacity for heavy industry, especially as the new Mill Plain Boulevard Extension eases freeway traffic west to the Port of Vancouver,

Recent downtown revitalization has created a hub for recreational and cultural events. Photos by Cliff Barbour

Market vendors enjoy a brisk business in the plaza of Esther Short Park. Photos by Cliff Barbour

unlocking development of Port lands and fortifying the economy with thousands of new jobs.

"We may not continue to grow at the current pace," Dearborn said, "but we need to grow, and we need to do it in a way that protects our environment. That means we're going to have to live closer together and be smarter about planning. Business plays a huge role in leadership and support for that effort. I see a community that's working closer together on creating a common vision of prosperity to maintain the quality of life that got us here in the first place."

That community turned out in force when Vancouver Farmers Market 2000 opened its 10th season at Esther Short Park. The market was a longtime fixture near the historic Evergreen Hotel a few blocks away, but new construction forced a move. The park, meanwhile, was being redone as the centerpiece of downtown revitalization—a community landmark and gathering place. The work was far from finished, but the market found a home near the new park plaza for at least two seasons, maybe more.

In April 2000 on a sunny Saturday, more than 5,000 people flocked to the plaza in a festive, barn-raising mood. They browsed the farm-fresh produce and handmade goods. They picnicked on the lawns while their children tried out the new playground. They strolled along the river, wandered through Vancouver's retail shops, and came back to the market to browse some more. Many vendors sold out before closing.

City officials were delighted. The day marked the informal debut of a newly livable downtown, and the crowds loved it. Through the summer the market racked up its most successful season ever. "The colorful lively market and the open green space of the park make the perfect blend," said market master Dawn Blankenship. "We hear that over and over again from our shoppers." Meanwhile, new apartments and retail clusters near the park are creating the central-city version of the kind of all-in-one neighborhood Steve Dearborn envisions. Esther Short Park has quickly become a model for older and new neighborhoods throughout the county.

At the same time, public and private partners are tending to the groundwork of prosperity as well as its infrastructure. In early 2000 the Vancouver-based Columbia Land Trust received nearly $1 million from the U.S. Fish & Wildlife Service—the largest such grant the agency has ever made. The Land Trust plans to acquire 1,500 acres of wetlands and upland habitat in the lower Columbia River basin and to restore and enhance 4,400 acres of salmon and waterfowl habitat.

Clark County's historical legacy, too, is being strongly championed. "We're very fortunate that the cultural landscape here is largely intact in a practical sense," said John Marshall, executive director of the Vancouver National Historic Reserve Trust. "There's something about walking around in it, seeing, feeling, sensing the history of this special place, that is very significant. Not a day goes by that you don't uncover another linkage."

Thousands attended the Farmers Market's opening day in Esther Short Park. Photo by Cliff Barbour

Mayor Royce Pollard put it this way: "We're going to create the premier historical site in the West. This is something for America, and we have it here in our community."

Before he became mayor, Pollard served in the U.S. Army, commanding Vancouver Barracks during his final tour of duty. He is the living embodiment of Vancouver's history of military and civilian partnership, and a zealous advocate for its preservation. Nevertheless, one chapter of that history in particular gives him pain.

In August 1877, as General Oliver O. Howard pursued Chief Joseph of the Nez Perce to his famous last stand in the Bear Paw Mountains of Montana, some of Joseph's band surrendered and were brought to Vancouver Barracks and held captive there through the winter. Their chief was Redheart. On April 22, 1878, they were taken by steamboat back up the river to the reservation at Lapwai, Idaho—22 men, nine women, and one child. They had reached the Barracks with two children, but one, an infant, had died.

Pollard was looking ahead to the Lewis and Clark Bicentennial when he came upon this story. He met with the Nez Perce, and the city invited the tribe to Vancouver for a ceremony of reconciliation. On April 22, 1998, Redheart's people returned to Vancouver Barracks for the first time in 120 years to honor the memory of their ancestors who had suffered there.

"We learned from them about the tribe's first encounter with Lewis and Clark," the mayor said. "They found them coming down the Bitterroot Valley, sick and dying. Some of the band wanted to kill them, but an old woman said to let them live. So they helped them and gave them food. The Nez Perce were responsible for the westernmost phase of Lewis and Clark's journey. If it weren't for them, we wouldn't be having this bicentennial."

The Nez Perce annually commemorate all the places where their people fought and perished. Vancouver was not a battle site, but they wanted to come here to honor Redheart's band. They came again the next year, bringing horses and other gifts for their hosts. In 2000, more tribes and members of the Native American Veterans

In 2000 the city of Vancouver paid tribute to members of the Nez Perce tribe who were held captive at the Vancouver Barracks from 1877 to 1878. Nez Perce representatives and members of the Native American Veterans joined in the ceremony, held at the Fort Vancouver Historic Reserve. A bench was dedicated to the captives, and aspens were planted in memory of a Nez Perce baby who died during the incarceration. Photos by Cliff Barbour

Association joined in the ceremony. The city dedicated a bench to the captives near the Veterans Memorial on the Reserve, planted quaking aspens in memory of the baby who died, and sent more trees home with the Nez Perce to Lapwai.

The ceremony does not gloss over what happened, but simply acknowledges it. "I just think it's the right thing to do," said the mayor. "I'm not proud of the Army's response. The Historic Reserve is intended to interpret layers of history, and with this reconciliation we are uncovering more layers. There are Nez Perce who love Vancouver now. I would hope that over the years, we would be able to build this into a congress of Native American tribes here in Vancouver for serious discussion of significant issues at a national level."

What's certain is that the people who long ago helped the Corps of Discovery make its way down the Columbia River will be part of Jim Demetro's new sculpture to commemorate the Bicentennial.

Like his vision of George Vancouver—and unlike any other work of its kind in the country—this sequential bronze rendering of the expedition will be the product of many hands. Anyone interested will have a chance to smooth a little clay onto the forms. Citizens will raise the money, and philanthropists will match it. The artist will donate much of his time. Children will learn about history through seeing, touching, discovering.

And years from now, when they come to Vancouver to show their own children where they added their bit of clay, they can say, "That's my spot!" *V*

Like the city that bears his name, the bronze figure of Captain George Vancouver awaits new discoveries. Photos by Cliff Barbour

Photo by Cliff Barbour

PART TWO

A Portrait of Prosperity

Transportation, Energy, & Communications

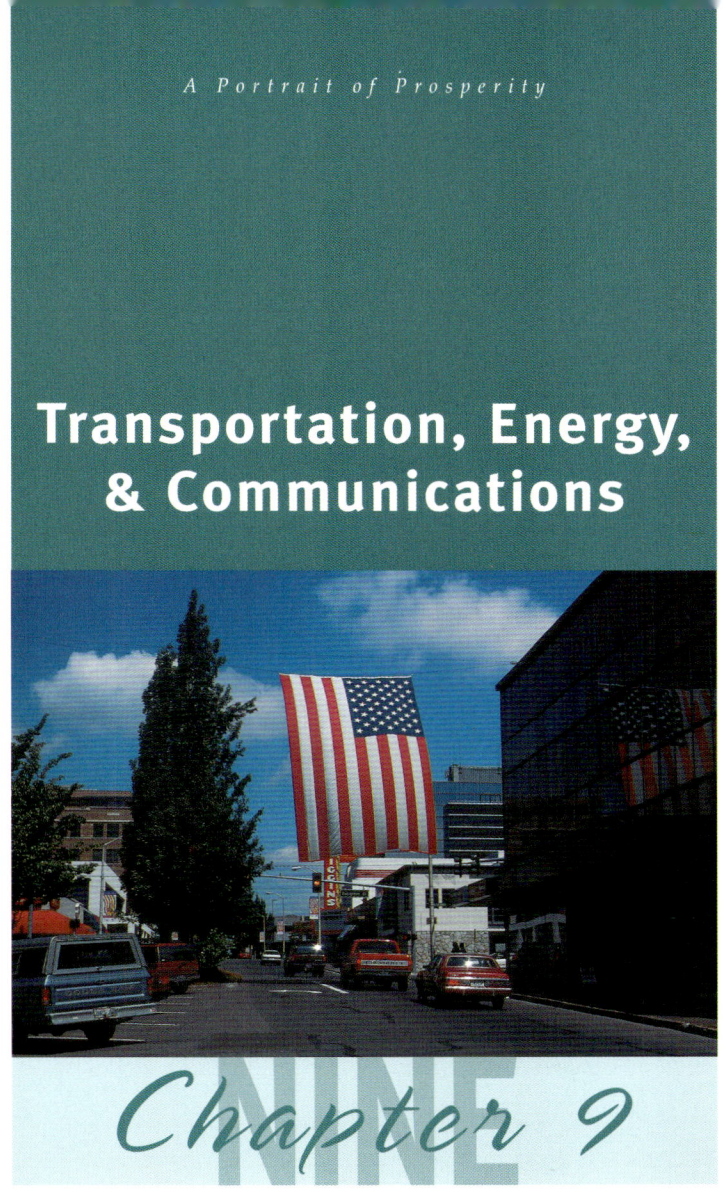

Chapter 9

Bonneville Power Administration, 96

Tidewater Barge Lines, Inc., 98

Ray Hickey: Hickey Family Company, 100

New Edge Networks, 102

Vancouver Business Journal, 104

Photos by Cliff Barbour

Bonneville Power Administration

The Pacific Northwest is blessed with an abundance of natural resources. The melting snow from the peaks of the Cascades and the annual rainfall helps fill its rivers and flows to the oceans in a cycle as old as time itself.

This cycle of nature also provides affordable electrical power to approximately eight million people in the Northwest—all of it flowing through a transmission grid owned by the Bonneville Power Administration. More than 15,000 miles of high-voltage lines move nearly 26-billion watts of power from federal, public, and private dams and power plants to cities and towns throughout the Northwest and beyond.

Who is responsible for making sure the power gets to where it needs to be? Who ensures the power stays on for homes and businesses? The employees at the Transmission Business Line headquartered in Vancouver. While the BPA's Portland-based power business sells electricity, the Vancouver group is responsible for operating, building, and maintaining the high-voltage electrical lines and substations.

These lines extend from the power sources along the Columbia River and its tributaries to substations throughout the region. The system reaches about 80 percent of the population of the Northwest, a responsibility the employees take very seriously. That's not surprising, considering the long history of dedication by the BPA to energize the region. Its roots go back to the Great Depression.

President Franklin D. Roosevelt was a driving force behind the development of hydroelectric power in the Northwest, giving the go-ahead for the Bonneville and Grand Coulee dams in 1933. In 1937, he signed the Bonneville Power Act that not only declared that the "facilities for the generation of electric energy . . . shall be operated for the benefit of the general public," but also created the Bonneville Power Administration to market and deliver the power.

The first 3.4 miles of transmission line were built in just over a week in 1938, and connected Cascade Locks, Oregon, to the just completed Bonneville Dam—a modest start in what soon became a multi-billion dollar investment in transmission facilities.

The BPA's mission was as clear then as it is today: To promote the widest possible use of electricity, to sell federal power at the lowest possible cost, to give preference in sales to municipal systems, public utilities, and rural and residential, and to build the necessary transmission system to accomplish those goals.

BPA's Vancouver-based transmission business owns more than 15,000 miles of high-voltage transmission line, moving 26 billion watts of power to about eight million people in the Northwest.

BPA is a self-financed agency. It pays for its costs through the sales of power and transmission. Bonneville was built in the Northwest to serve the Northwest, which is why residents benefit from electricity rates that are among the lowest in the western U.S.

In 1992, the National Energy Policy Act deregulated the electric utility industry. Federal regulators wanted high-voltage transmission facilities organized into regional grids to act as common carriers for power. Across the nation, integrated electric utilities split their operations into separate power generating and transmission businesses. Thus, Transmission Business Line (TBL) was born.

Today, building and maintaining the transmission grid remains the purpose of TBL and Dittmer Control Center in Vancouver, located at the 225-acre Ross Complex. TBL owns 80 percent of the Northwest's high-voltage transmission capacity.

Lines now span rivers and mountains, tying together dams and load centers of major cities like Portland, Seattle, and Spokane. The system is comprised of more than 40,000 steel towers and 76,000 wood poles connecting 385 substations throughout the region.

BPA is more than megawatts. It has been part of the economic health of the region's towns and industries for more than six decades.

Inter-regional transmission lines and strategic partnerships means TBL can connect to any point throughout the West, buying, selling, or exchanging power from Canada to New Mexico.

Those at Dittmer dispatch the BPA system, making sure that the power supply is in correct balance with the demand. Like "traffic cops," they move millions of kilowatts of electricity through the grid efficiently and monitor load to prevent backups. With 350 customers and up to 2,500 transmission schedules every day, that's no easy task.

Dispatchers use a highly sophisticated computer system to constantly stay in touch to see how any part of the system is working and make adjustments as necessary. Whether it's mother nature or human nature disrupting power, the people at Dittmer can respond instantly, pinpointing the problem and rerouting the flow of power. Most of the time, consumers don't even know there's been a problem. And when there is an outage, dispatch, field service crews, and support teams restore power quickly and safely.

BPA's Transmission Business Line has also been the leader and innovator in finding ways to help customers gain access to the transmission system. Through its Open Access Same-time Information System (OASIS), BPA became the first public agency to offer an on-line reservation system that guarantees non-discriminatory access to all. Users can reserve capacity 24 hours a day through the Internet and know that they are getting the same price and capacity information as other users.

But not all of TBL's 865 Vancouver employees operate and dispatch the grid system. Employees at the Transmission Headquarters also handle marketing, accounts, and customer service; plan ways to meet future demands for service; study operations to make sure the system stays safe and reliable no matter what happens; test much of the equipment used to deliver power; and train apprentices to

Reliable service is second only to safety. BPA's transmission grid has some of the best reliability statistics in the nation—and a history of rapid response in emergencies.

On line in real time, Dittmer dispatchers keep the power flowing 24 hours a day, every day.

operate the grid and all electrical workers in safety procedures to handle high voltage. There are also linemen who climb the 150-foot towers to do a "highwire" act—sometimes in the middle of night or during ice storms—just to keep the electricity flowing.

The Ross Complex also houses a warehouse with more than $30-million dollars in inventory—from multi-million dollar transformers to circuit breakers, everything necessary to build and maintain the region's substations.

Employees at TBL have a strong work ethic—they know their job is to "keep the lights on." But they find time to contribute to the community, as well. Most employees live in the Vancouver area and volunteer with organizations such as Boy Scouts. They work with schools to support science, safety, and environmental programs.

A group of employees calling themselves the Ross Canyon Social Club sponsor the annual visit from Santa Claus for children from the East Vancouver Child Care Center. And BPA turned an old home near its Ross Complex into a community meeting space for the West Minnehaha Neighborhood Association.

What does the future hold? The Federal Energy Regulatory Commission recently proposed forming Regional Transmission Organizations (RTO) across America. The FERC believes an RTO could improve transmission grid management, reliability, and market performance. With more than 15,000 miles of transmission lines, BPA's Transmission Business Line—with its Vancouver facilities—is sure to be a player.

Delivering the electricity that drives the Northwest—that's what the BPA and the Transmission Business Line are all about now, and will continue to be well into the future.

Tidewater Barge Lines, Inc.

SERVICE, PRIDE, INTEGRITY, SINCE 1932

Tidewater, headquartered in Vancouver, Washington, is the largest inland marine transportation company west of the Mississippi River, providing connections for truck, rail, and waterborne freight throughout the Pacific Northwest and beyond. With an integrated system of towboats, barges, and terminal facilities operating 24 hours a day, 365 days a year, Tidewater moves the region's commodities, including over 10 percent of all U.S. export wheat.

Founded in 1932, Tidewater began with steam-powered sternwheelers to haul the materials and machinery that helped to build the Pacific Northwest—concrete for dams, asphalt for roads, pipe for irrigation, fertilizer for agriculture. The company's history mirrors the record of modern innovations in marine shipping, as its equipment, terminals, and facilities have kept pace with changes in worldwide transportation.

Today, Tidewater is a proud Clark County community partner. The Tidewater name, a familiar feature of the rugged Northwest landscape, has become nationally known for technological and service advances that have helped expand the marine transportation industry.

(above) Providing economic transportation which allows the region to compete in the world market.

(below left) A proud Clark County partner in protecting the environment of the Pacific Northwest.

Tidewater helps sustain Clark County's economy and ecology by operating efficiently and conscientiously, providing high-wage jobs, and demonstrating concern and care for the community and environment. The company serves the Northwest region from Astoria, Oregon, at the mouth of the Columbia, to the Portland harbor at the mouth of the Willamette River, to the Port of Lewiston at the confluence of the Snake and Clearwater Rivers in Idaho. Its reach thus extends from the Pacific Ocean to the heart of the most productive wheat-growing land in the United States.

Petroleum products arrive in Portland via ship, ocean barge, and pipeline, where Tidewater loads them onto barges, then transports and stores them at its upstream facilities to provide fuel for inland communities. Wheat and feed grains, agricultural and forest products, manufactured goods, and other commodities are barged back downriver for worldwide export from Portland, Vancouver, and other Lower Columbia ports.

Because barges move 15 percent of the country's total freight at two percent of total transportation costs (one barge carries as much grain as 35 rail cars or 120 trucks), marine transportation can maintain this vital link between the Columbia/Snake River region and the global marketplace at top efficiency. Tidewater is proud of its role in keeping shipping costs down and thus giving the Pacific Northwest a competitive edge in the world market.

A Portrait of Prosperity

Tidewater is committed to improving the livability and environmental health of the Pacific Northwest. For example, Tidewater began construction and operation of double-hulled petroleum barges a full 20 years before required by federal regulation. Anticipating regulations to control the release of gasoline vapors into the environment, Tidewater also installed vapor-recovery systems on those barges as well.

Besides investing in equipment, Tidewater also invests in its employees. The company continuously trains its staff in environmental safety, conducts company-wide spill-response and pollution-prevention programs, and maintains a high-level emergency-response team.

Tidewater is a member of the American Waterways Operators Association and a certified AWO Responsible Carrier because of its safety awareness and environmental stewardship. Through training and awareness, Tidewater people and equipment stand ready to meet any problem all along the river system. The prime focus is always to keep the natural environment pristine and pure.

Tidewater employees are active community partners.

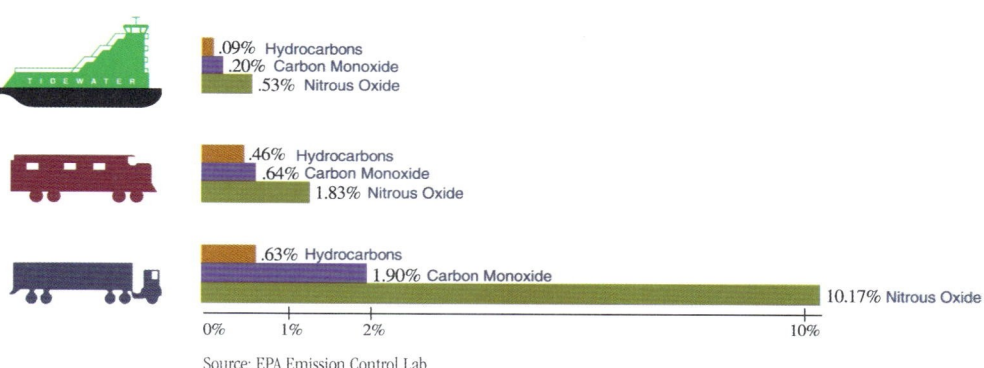

Barging is kind to the environment...
Inland marine transportation minimizes fuel emissions per ton of cargo.

Source: EPA Emission Control Lab

Tidewater people are consistent and reliable, bringing company values of commitment and service to every job, and giving every customer, large and small, their full attention. Customers can count on intermodal connections, prompt deliveries, coordinated shipping and storage, and consolidated freight services all along the route. Tidewater people helped build Tidewater's well-earned reputation, and each of them takes personal responsibility for carrying it forward. No matter who responds to a call, customers always know they're working with Tidewater.

Much more than a barge line, Tidewater is expanding into the future, keeping its promises, transcending what it has done before. It has earned the trust and respect of its customers and communities by maintaining the highest levels of service, professionalism, ethics, and integrity. New customers who are drawn to Tidewater by its excellent reputation find a dynamic full-service company wide open to new possibilities.

GUIDING PRINCIPLES OF OPERATIONS

The people of Tidewater respect the privilege of operating on the waterways of the Pacific Northwest. Together they accept responsibility for adhering to these guiding principles:
- We will maintain safe operations which meet or exceed all regulatory and industry established standards.
- We will operate in a manner that protects our communities, our environment and our customers.
- We will strive to maintain a leadership position within our industry through constant innovation and improvement.
- We will earn the trust and respect of our customers and our communities by maintaining the highest levels of service, professionalism, ethics, and integrity.
- We will achieve excellence by accepting responsibility and accountability for the actions of ourselves and our co-workers, while fostering a working environment of growth, encouragement, and respect.

The people of Tidewater are proud of their heritage and are committed to operating in a manner that enhances the livability of the Pacific Northwest for future generations.

Ray Hickey
Hickey Family Company

As Clark County continues to grow and evolve, residents marvel at their ability to stay in touch with nature in the midst of new development. Thanks to one Vancouver businessman with a vision and dedication for giving back to the community, many are now enjoying the chance to reacquaint themselves with the waterfront along the Columbia River.

Ray Hickey donated part of his company's waterfront property to build a three-and-a-quarter-mile trail along the waterfront promenade. Joggers, walkers, bicyclists, and families have a stunning view of the river and the Portland skyline as they travel along the public trail.

All people can enjoy this view because Hickey, who made his career from the river, believes that the waterfront belongs to the community, and he understands that people need to "be able to come down and touch the river." This philanthropic attitude led Hickey to start with the gift of his own property to make this dream come true.

Ray Hickey's name is a familiar one to those in Clark County, and nearly synonymous with the barge industry, although he has never sought publicity for his business or charitable works.

His association with the river began in 1951, when he landed a deckhand job with Tidewater Barge Lines. Within a year he was chief engineer on the largest tug on the Columbia River, until 1955, when he was transferred to the Ocean division. There he expanded his horizons, moving products to California, Hawaii, and Alaska, as well as being involved in several trips through the Panama Canal.

By 1970, he was brought back to the river to help shape Tidewater's future operations and eventually, its policies. In 1975, Hickey built the first modern towboat on the river since the 1940s—the 3,000-hp Captain Bob. By 1977, he was president of Tidewater Barge Lines. He actively helped the company grow through the acquisition of Sundial Marine Shipyard and Repair on the Columbia River. And in 1983, in the midst of a national recession and falling grain prices, Hickey took the first of several key steps in solidifying Tidewater's future by purchasing the company.

During the mid-1980s, Hickey further bought out major competitors Knappton and Columbia Marine Lines in significant acquisitions that defined both him and his company as major players in the country's tug and barge industry.

Hickey continued to expand his business, adding petroleum terminals, container yards, and Columbia Resource Company, a solid waste entity which included a transfer station network and a state-of-the-art landfill.

In addition, Hickey's unique vision of vertically integrating marine services accounted for the development of Hickey Marine Enterprises, which builds and repairs docks and handles river dredging, and Tidewater Environmental Services. It consisted of operating procedures, trained personnel, and response equipment prepared to act immediately in the event of an oil or other river spill.

Most of the adjacent businesses Hickey started have been sold, and in 1996, he sold Tidewater to a select group of investors that included his son, Wesley J. Hickey. But at a

(top) Looking out on the Columbia River is a man with a vision, Ray Hickey. © 2000 Dan Bronson.

(left) Ray's beliefs etched in stone. © 2000 Dan Bronson.

time when most men are planning retirement, Hickey began to actively develop a plan that he had first envisioned in the mid-1970s.

Seeing the decline of industrial activity along the Columbia waterfront above the Interstate 5 bridge, Hickey began thinking about finding a way to give people more access to the water. He never gave up his initial dream of developing the Tidewater acreage for housing, business, and public access.

By 1987, the time was right, and the community, civic leaders, and government teamed up to take action on the project. Aided by his daughter, Linda Hickey, Ray Hickey had his barge headquarters and operations moved downriver creating a new waterfront at a personal cost of $9 million.

In 1999, another step in his dream was realized when Hickey donated 51 acres of property to the City of Vancouver for wetlands, tidelands, and a public trail system. The city donated nearly $500,000 for the waterfront trail extension from the Marine Park upriver through the Tidewater property to Wintler Park.

Thirty-seven acres of former Hickey property is being developed. In all, Tidewater Cove will be a $120-million mixed-use development that could include 100-plus town-home condominiums, and waterfront condominiums, and 50,000 to 70,000 square feet of office space. Also envisioned is a commercial development that includes a restaurant, marina, and a small amphitheater.

Hickey's donation to the city of Vancouver is very much in keeping with his philosophy of giving back. Hickey was consciously contributing to the community with the Boy Scouts and Little League even when he was at the point where he had nothing to give but his time. And as he has acquired resources, Hickey has set an example of charitable giving for his neighbors in Clark County. The Diabetes and Heart Associations, the American Red Cross, Doernbecher Children's Hospital, and the YWCA and YMCA all have benefited from Hickey's generosity.

Most recently, he stepped up to endow the Celebrate Freedom program, a series of events and lectures that highlight Vancouver's place in history. Hickey's $1.5-million matching-endowment pledge will ensure that Vancouver residents continue to celebrate their heritage for generations to come.

In 1997, Ray Hickey was named First Citizen of the Year by the Community Foundation for Southwest Washington. He was uniformly praised by public officials and private business owners alike for his volunteerism, leadership, and service to the community.

A successful businessman, environmentalist, charitable benefactor—these are all words to describe a man who has left a legacy of generosity and appreciation of nature to the community. The Ray Hickey Family Company and the riverfront project will continue to be an important influence on the Clark County community for generations to come.

(top) Ray Hickey flanked by a painting of his tugs—"The Fleet of Dreams." © 2000 Dan Bronson.

(below) A run with a view along the waterfront trail. © 2000 Dan Bronson.

New Edge Networks

In the warp-speed world of new technology, there's the front, the forefront, and the outer edge, a place where only brave visionaries dare to venture. New Edge Networks is there.

The nation's leading wholesale broadband services provider for small, midsize, and semi-rural markets, New Edge Networks is using its DSL (digital subscriber line) technology to take high-speed Internet connections to Americans often left in the "back waters" of progress simply because of where they choose to live.

Just a few short years ago, sending e-mail was the primary function for just about anyone with an Internet connection. Fully developed commercial Web sites were few and slow to access at best. Now, the World Wide Web is mainstream for conducting e-business, viewing streaming video, listening to music or the radio, building company intranets, and on-line commercial shopping, where you can order anything from clothes to cars.

In addition, the Internet is bringing a new learning, communication, and social dynamic to everyone from kids and teenagers to older Americans seeking to connect with far-flung families, friends, and interests. Hold onto your mouse, more benefits are around the corner and will need delivery speeds to match.

New Edge Networks connects homes, businesses, and corporate data networks to the Internet using existing telephone lines that are up to 100 times faster than a typical dial-up analog modem. So when you go to a Web site using an "always-on" connection from New Edge Networks, there's little waiting and the page downloads virtually instantly. This allows people to do more on line, and be more productive in their personal as well as professional lives.

Another benefit to DSL's "always-on" connection is that it gives businesses a distinct competitive advantage. For business customers with dedicated leased lines from local telephone companies, DSL technology generally provides the same speed at half the monthly cost. And, as technology advances and costs come down, DSL service becomes an even more compelling business requirement.

Founded in June 1999, New Edge Networks grew from five co-founders to more than 400 associates in barely one year. The company established one of the fastest-to-market benchmarks for offering this breakthrough service—120 days. Its plan: to have a national network providing DSL service through partnerships with local, regional, and national Internet Service Providers and communications companies in all 50 states within 18 months of starting.

The goal of New Edge Networks is to bridge the digital divide with technology, but behind that are customer-focused people who care about smaller communities and bringing the same advantages to these people that their big-city cousins have. The co-founders, headed by Dan Moffat, president and CEO, also have a passion to build the most desirable company at which to work.

From a corporate culture point-of-view, New Edge Networks is not your typical company. In fact, "corporate" is referred to as the "loop factory." The founders are building on an environment where people are comfortable expressing ideas and empowered to carry them out. You won't find the usual kind of office hierarchy, either. No plush, private offices anywhere in the building. From the CEO to the newest employee, everyone works in open cubicles. The only spaces with doors are conference rooms.

And you won't find your typical work areas at New Edge Networks, either. Rather than hire a decorator and have a uniform vanilla look, each work team took a budget and came up with their own decorating scheme. The result: a Hawaiian motif alongside classic white pillars supporting reflecting garden globes and a Star Wars theme; state flags hanging from the ceiling; and themes range from jungle to tropical, nautical, and '70s disco to a "New Edge City" and cartoon land. It's a casual, yet creative and very high-energy atmosphere that reflects the nature of New Edge's associates and their mission.

"We work hard and we play hard." That's the mantra at New Edge Networks. Every Friday at 4:30, Moffat rings a school hand-bell and everyone gathers for a well-deserved break and celebration of the week's accomplishments, introduction of new employees, and just socializing. And, Hawaiian shirts—the gaudier the better—dominate the scene.

But that's not all in this new world culture. There are toys and gadgets everywhere, and ping-pong and foosball tables for "down" time. And every New Edge Networks associate has a stake through stock options.

New Edge Networks calls Vancouver its home because the founders—reflecting the people the company serves in small, midsize, and semi-rural areas nationwide—choose to live in this area and are proud of the community, its people, lifestyle, and resources. The company is bringing new opportunities to the Vancouver community, as well as broadening the bedrock of technology-based companies in the Northwest. Founders and associates are dedicated to building a great company that will continue to thrive and contribute to the region's future success.

New Edge Networks is located at 3000 Columbia House Boulevard, Vancouver, WA 98661. For more information call 360-906-9009 or visit the company's Web site at www.newedgenetworks.com.

A Portrait of Prosperity

"We work hard and we play hard." That's the mantra at New Edge Networks. Every Friday at 4:30, Dan Moffat, president and CEO, rings a school hand-bell and everyone gathers for a well-deserved break and celebration of the week's accomplishments. Photo by Cliff Barbour.

Vancouver Business Journal

From one man's dream, begun in his garage, to a thriving paper that keeps Clark County businesses up-to-date on business news. That's the story of the *Vancouver Business Journal*.

Founded in 1994, the *Vancouver Business Journal* started out as a free monthly newspaper, but quickly grew to a bi-weekly. It also began publishing supplemental magazines, such as the *Book of Lists*, the *Business Women's Journal*, *Northwest Greens Golf Guide*, *Welcome to Clark County*, and *Business Resource Guide*.

In 1998, Dolan Media Co. of Minneapolis, Minnesota, purchased the *Vancouver Business Journal*. Dolan Media Co. is a national specialized business information company that publishes business and court and commercial newspapers and other print and electronic media products serving the law, credit, finance, construction, and commercial real estate markets.

Now on the threshold of a new millennium, the *Vancouver Business Journal* celebrated the year 2000 by going to weekly publication. It also began paid circulation for the first time—$42 dollars for 52 weeks.

The *Vancouver Business Journal* provides the best and most in-depth Clark County business news coverage. The *VBJ* reports on everything going on in the community that has the potential to affect local businesses.

Inside every issue of the *Vancouver Business Journal*, is not only the latest business news, but also community news, such as the awarding of a grant or who's contributing to a foundation. Also included are reviews on business books, investment news, and marketing tips.

The *Vancouver Business Journal* also features a business and events calendar, real estate and development news, and company rankings for specific industries.

In addition to the news coverage and the company profiles, there are articles by financial experts and advisors, by management consultants, and any number of people who are top-rated experts in their fields. Plus, "how-to" articles, which many of the smaller businesses say they've come to depend on. It's almost like having a business consultant without the high fees. No wonder research shows the paper is "passed around" in offices, so that for every one subscriber, there are at least five readers.

The *Vancouver Business Journal* boasts a sophisticated graphics staff, an editor, assistant editor, and two reporters, along with four professional advertising consultants and two friendly, helpful office employees. Every week, all employees work to bring readers what's timely, what's interesting, or perhaps a unique angle on an existing story.

The *Vancouver Business Journal* focuses on a company at its best. In fact, that's part of the mission statement: "Keep businesses informed and help them succeed."

With a beat that includes Vancouver, Clark County, Camas, Washougal, and Ridgefield, the *Vancouver Business Journal* is proud to call itself the "Local voice for Vancouver and Clark County business."

The *Vancouver Business Journal* doesn't just cover the area, it contributes to it as well, by sponsoring events such as the Relay for Life for cancer, the Columbia River Charity golf tournament, and Art and Soul, Vancouver's Arts Festival.

The paper also sponsors the *Vancouver Business Journal* Business Fair and Trade Show. With 150 vendors participating, this "business-to-business" show is just one more way the paper serves the region.

A community paper dealing with community issues. That's the *Vancouver Business Journal*.

Vancouver Business Journal's *management team, from left: Shawn Williams, regional creative director; Jacquelyn Agee, publisher; Theresa Baer, editor; and Cheryl Smith, office manager.*

A Portrait of Prosperity

Photo by Cliff Barbour

A Portrait of Prosperity

Technology, Manufacturing, & Distribution

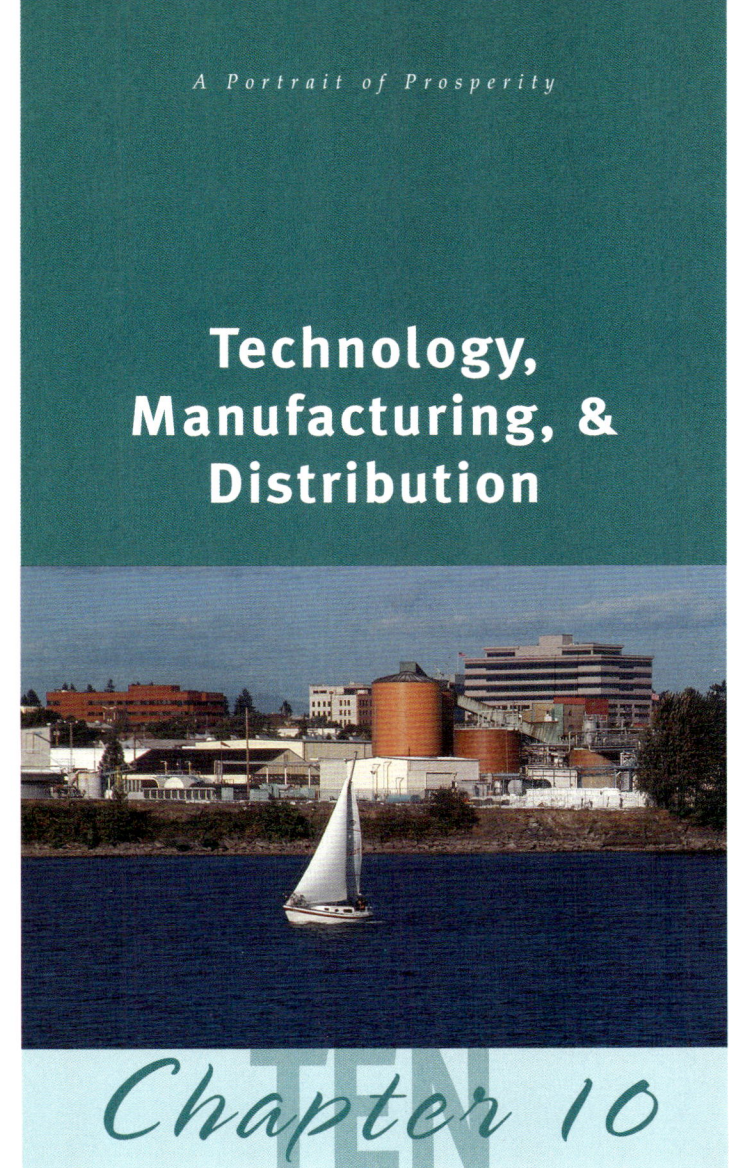

Chapter 10

Sharp, 108

Underwriters Laboratories Inc. of Camas, 110

Boise Cascade, 112

WaferTech, 114

Kyocera Industrial Ceramics Corporation, 115

ConAgra Malt: Great Western Malting Company, 116

Photos by Cliff Barbour

Sharp

SHARP MICROELECTRONICS OF THE AMERICAS

There are few products in American homes and businesses today that don't contain some sort of microelectronic component. Computers, cell phones, and pagers are becoming not luxuries, but commonplace throughout society. The explosive growth of the Internet and the World Wide Web is driving demand for all kinds of electronic devices, especially those that are portable and wireless, that can access this global network of information, entertainment, and services. And it's increasingly likely that all of these electronic devices, will be making life easier, thanks in part to Sharp Microelectronics of the Americas (SMA).

Located in Camas and sharing a 120-acre campus with Sharp Labs overlooking the scenic Columbia River, Sharp Microelectronics of the Americas is a forward-thinking company that is bringing the future right into homes with its wide array of integrated circuits, liquid crystal displays, optoelectronics, and RF components. In addition to sales and marketing responsibilities for components in North, Central, and South America, SMA capabilities include IC design, packaging, and system level integration.

Sharp prides itself in having a broad-based and diversified microelectronic product line with world leadership positions in many areas. It's been the leader in optoelectronic technologies for nearly two decades, sourcing more optoelectronic devices worldwide than any other manufacturer.

Sharp prides itself in the sincere and dedicated pursuit of new markets. Sharp is a creative company, using its ingenuity to broaden the spectrum of current products. A clear example of this philosophy can be seen in its Liquid Crystal Display (LCD) products. A pioneer in this field since the early 1970s, Sharp's continual need to improve and innovate has made it the recognized world leader in flat-panel

SMA headquarters sits on a 120-acre campus overlooking the scenic Columbia River, and is home to over 250 of Sharp's greatest assets—its employees.

System on Chip (SOC) design and development is a key focus area for Sharp.

displays, and the growth for this product is phenomenal. Laptop computers used to be heavy and bulky with screens that were difficult to see clearly. Thanks to Sharp's LCD technology, mobile PCs are lighter, larger, clearer, and more energy efficient. Handheld internet appliances and cell phones now boast color screens with crystal clear images. The flat-panel televisions in family mini-vans and the movie screens that flip down on airplanes are all made possible because of Sharp's advancements in LCD products. And someday soon everyone's digital television set will hang on the wall like a picture, mere inches thick.

Two of SMA's focus areas for the future are System On Chip (SOC) and Microcontroller Unit (MCU) development—the electronic brains that control virtually every electronic device. These products do the work of a dozen integrated circuits making the continued miniaturization of computers and other equipment possible, as well as the ability to access the internet anytime and anywhere.

Sharp sees tremendous growth opportunity in helping customers with system level integration, such as combining a SOC/MCU device, an LCD, and other peripheral components into modules for any number of applications, from cell phones to appliances.

Sharp is also one of the largest manufacturers of flash memory in the world. Flash is a key component in every cell phone. Forecasted growth for wireless communications with more features and functions is very strong, offering fantastic potential for Sharp.

Sharp Microelectronics of the Americas is a major employer in southwest Washington, with over 250 employees in Camas. SMA is a firm believer that its greatest asset is its employees and takes pride in fostering an employee culture and attitude upon which everything depends. Success comes directly from these dedicated and empowered employees, who take ownership in the company's direction and decisions, pride in their work, and share the vision of creating leading-edge products. They know the sky's the limit. The new millennium brings demand for technological innovation that is insatiable and brings with it a need for employees with new ideas and the ability to implement them. Sharp has those employees focused on implementing the company's vision and that's why Sharp Microelectronics of the Americas turns so optimistically to the future.

The products of the future are only a dream away, and Sharp will help bring them to the market.

SHARP LABS OF AMERICA

Where is society going? What are the needs of the American family? And what can be created to make their lives easier? These are the kinds of questions the researchers of Sharp Labs of America ask themselves every day.

Located in Camas, Sharp Labs is right next to Sharp Microelectronics of the Americas. Together, they bring ideas to fruition quickly in today's competitive technological environment.

Sharp Labs' motto is "Creating products that make a difference in people's lives." With that in mind, employees are constantly challenging themselves to invent, modify, and apply technologies in all areas that Sharp has expertise.

Sharp Labs does research in six departments: Digital Video, Multimedia Communications, Digital Imaging, Mobile Computing, Integrated Circuits (IC) processing, and Liquid Crystal Display (LCD) processing.

In Digital Video, Sharp Labs is continuing to improve high definition television (HDTV) and data services for interactive television. But Sharp Labs is also exploring technology to transmit digitally compressed video through a phone line, and improve displayed images to get a better picture on handheld or laptop computers or television projectors.

Bringing technology right to people's palms is the goal of multimedia communications research. The day is coming when all of one's personal communication services will be met in a hand-held device, from phone and fax, to web pads and full-motion video. With more people traveling on the job, Sharp Labs knows there's a tremendous need to develop products to help them do their jobs better while outside the office.

Printing, faxing, scanning, and copying—all these typical office activities are ready to move into the next generation of technology. Sharp's work in the area of Digital Imaging will enable offices to integrate different office machines into one next-generation product connected to a network or Internet. The transition from print and distribute to distribute and print is being accelerated by the availability of complex electronic documents.

"Creating products that make a difference in people's lives" is the motto of the researchers at Sharp Labs of America.

Sharp's breadth of microelectronic components makes it a strong global competitor.

Mobile computing is now standard in the U.S. However, new technologies and user interactions are being introduced by Sharp Labs in such areas as ease of use and the "out of box" experience.

Sharp Labs has the leading technology in the U.S. when it comes to Liquid Crystal Display (LCD) process. Whether it's being used in a hand-held digital video camera or the newest and smallest laptop computer, LCD is an area where Sharp Labs is a leader in innovation.

Much of this technology wouldn't be possible without the integrated circuit. Sharp Labs is on the cutting edge of this field, allowing products to become smaller and smarter all the time. But researchers are already looking at the generation beyond the next generation—to develop the IC technology for products that people haven't even discovered they need yet!

However, Sharp Labs doesn't push technology just for technology's sake, but to solve real problems and create products that have true potential to improve lives. That's why its watchwords are "Creativity and Sincerity."

Sharp Labs prides itself on allowing employees to be as creative as possible with far-reaching ideas. Sharing ideas is paramount to Sharp Labs, and employees know that this is an open place to work, where information is a team effort. This work culture is one reason why Sharp has been able to attract the far-sighted employees it has, and why it continues to be a company that develops new and exciting technologies for Sharp products.

People with a vision and the ability to see it through. That's what makes Sharp Labs of America a company that truly makes a difference in people's lives.

Underwriters Laboratories Inc. of Camas

As trade barriers continue to fall, the need for global conformity assessment services has increased. How can a consumer know whether a food processor manufactured in China will be as safe as one made in the United States? To answer this question, smart consumers know they only need to look for the Underwriters Laboratories' certification Mark—the familiar UL in a circle that indicates the product has met established and respected standards for safety.

A world leader in conformity assessment services, UL has had an impact on product safety for more than a century—ever since it developed standards for electrical wiring in 1894. William Henry Merrill founded UL and advanced the principles that continue today:
- Test for public safety, where the only function is to serve, not to profit.
- Know by test and state the facts.

The initial lab Merrill set up in Chicago performed 75 tests in its first year, at a cost of $3,000. Today, more than 16 billion UL Marks appear on more than 18,000 types of products annually. UL tests products for manufacturers in 89 countries and has 193 inspection centers in 71 countries, as well as five full-service testing labs in the United States, including Camas, Washington.

UL's Camas facility is one of five U.S locations testing products as part of UL's commitment to public safety.

Established in 1994 with only 12 employees, UL's Camas facility now boasts a staff of more than 200 at its 116,000-square-foot facility, which is beautifully situated on 72 acres near Lacamas Lake. A visitor walking around the facility will see technicians and engineers putting products through their paces. It may look a bit odd to see a

As part of UL's electromagnetic compatibility testing, products such as computers, microwave ovens, and medical devices are evaluated for emission levels of radiation and their susceptibility to interference.

machine twisting extension cords for a week or more, or space heaters running for days on end, or items dropped from great heights, but it's all in the name of safety.

UL strives to answer two important questions: Does the product function safely? And if or when it does fail, does it fail safely? Simply, products either meet the criterion set by standards, or the manufacturer doesn't get permission to use the world-recognized UL Mark.

UL's technicians and engineers believe there can be no acceptable compromises or shortcuts where safety is concerned. In fact, UL is the backbone of the U.S. Safety System, literally writing the book on safety standards for 748 products—everything from air conditioning equipment to hairdryers to x-ray equipment used in hospitals and doctors' offices.

UL standards are developed and authored in an open process that encourages input from all interested parties, including representatives from government agencies, insurance companies, code authorities, medical experts, consumer groups, and manufacturers. As part of the standard development and revision process, UL standards are continually updated or revised with new requirements to proactively keep pace with advancements in technologies and how products are being used.

The Camas facility is ideally situated for companies in the Pacific Northwest that want their products tested. It's also the jumping-off point for Asia, and with ever-expanding trade in that part of the world, the UL Mark becomes the *entreé* for international companies to sell to America. There is strong incentive to earn the UL Mark; in many cases, retailers simply won't sell a product and code authorities won't let products be installed if they do not bear the UL Mark.

By the same token, American products shipped overseas have to meet the strict standards of each specific country. UL has developed a specialty in electromagnetic compatibility (or EMC) testing for emitters such as computers, video displays, and disc drives. UL's tests confirm that a product not only meets strict FCC levels for the United States, but those of the International Electrotechnical Community, also known as the IEC.

Proud of its open style of management and positive employee culture, UL sizzles with enthusiasm for what it does. Everyone at the Camas facility knows their work is more than just punching the clock from nine to five. They realize it is a mission. They know what they do affects lives around the globe. There's truly a sense of pride in knowing they are part of the process that makes safe products available the world over.

UL is not only a major employer in the region, but its employees also serve on numerous community groups dealing with everything from education and economic development to the local environment. UL wants to be more than just a good place to work, but a good neighbor as well. Local teachers and school children of all ages have the opportunity to tour the facility year-round, learning the importance of product safety.

Although the Camas facility tests a variety of products, from household appliances to space heaters to hot tubs, it does a great deal of testing on wire and cable. More than 3,500 various styles of wire and cable have been tested and certified by UL. Since the average 2,200-square-foot home has more than 3,000 feet of wire, it is critical that the wire has been evaluated for safety.

And to make sure it is installed correctly, UL's Camas facility offers workshops and classes to electricians, code authorities,

As part of the evaluation of a plastic material used to make a product enclosure, a UL technician selectively burns away portions of the material.

inspection officials, and others in the building construction industry. In fact, the facility has more than 2,000 square feet of classroom space available for its employees and local safety professionals. It also makes educational offerings available for companies wishing to learn how to design their products from the ground up to meet UL standards. There are programs and UL services to help companies meet specific management system registration needs such as ISO 9000, ISO 14001, TL-9000, and QS-9000. By meeting these internationally recognized, quality standards, manufacturers have a better chance of marketing their products in the global marketplace.

Even after a product earns the UL mark for safety, UL's work is not done. UL conducts random visits to manufacturing facilities throughout the world several times a year to verify that products coming off the production line continue to meet UL's requirements. To give some perspective, as part of its follow-up service program UL conducted more than 509,000 product audits in more than 58,000 different factories in 1999 alone.

A global vision with local action. That's UL. From its Camas facility to its 46 subsidiaries and affiliates throughout the world, UL never compromises on safety. For more than 106 years, UL has set the standard for safety and will continue to do so beyond the 21st century.

By testing the physical properties of wire insulation, UL confirms that wire and cable will maintain its resilience over long periods of time.

Boise Cascade

Most people have probably never taken a close look at the paper on which their bank checks are printed. But if they did, they might be surprised to learn how unique that kind of paper is. And they might be even more surprised to learn that the paper likely came from a Boise Cascade plant in Vancouver.

What was once a typical paper mill is now a specialty paper plant that has seen remarkable growth since setting up shop. The Vancouver mill, a 37.5-acre industrial site located along the Columbia River, has a long history in the Pacific Northwest, having been founded by F. W. Leadbetter in 1922. In 1962, it was purchased by Boise Cascade Corporation, and through the years has seen many changes.

The mill's wood room and pulp mill ceased operation in 1969. Recycled content paper production started in 1991, using virgin pulp from its St. Helens mill and recycled content pulp of its own. Finally came the change that brought about today's current production facility.

It was 1996 when Boise Cascade decided to discontinue manufacturing paper completely at its Vancouver plant. But rather than let the property sit idle, or sell it, the company decided to convert the plant to specialized printing jobs. The first step in manufacturing these "value added" papers, is ordinary paper, which comes from the St. Helens, Oregon paper mill. Then it's converted into security papers and coated papers for inkjet printers.

The high-tech security papers are destined to become checks, bank certificates, bonds, and other papers for the banking industry. Some of them are extremely "high-tech" to avoid fraud, with features like incandescent fibers and special registered patterns.

Another anti-fraud technique is chemically reactive paper, which signals attempts to alter or remove the laser-printed word.

Today's criminals are able to use desktop printers to create fraudulent documents, and more and more businesses depend on these special papers to give them the security they need. Boise's security paper products help make it tougher for counterfeiters and forgers to make such things as fake checks, bonds, or even tickets to sporting events.

The increased incidents of fraud have definitely driven the market. The securities papers market is growing very rapidly, up to 10 percent a year. That compares to a two to three percent growth for regular paper sales.

When the paper mill was shut down in 1996, the Vancouver Boise plant was left with two security papers printing presses and one paper-coating machine. But the growth in the security paper industry has led to growth at

(top) Jeff Howard changes paper slitters on the Kidder machine, which prints check protect paper.

(below) Jeff Galloway puts air into the shaft of the Arrow paper window at Boise Cascade's Vancouver Specialties.

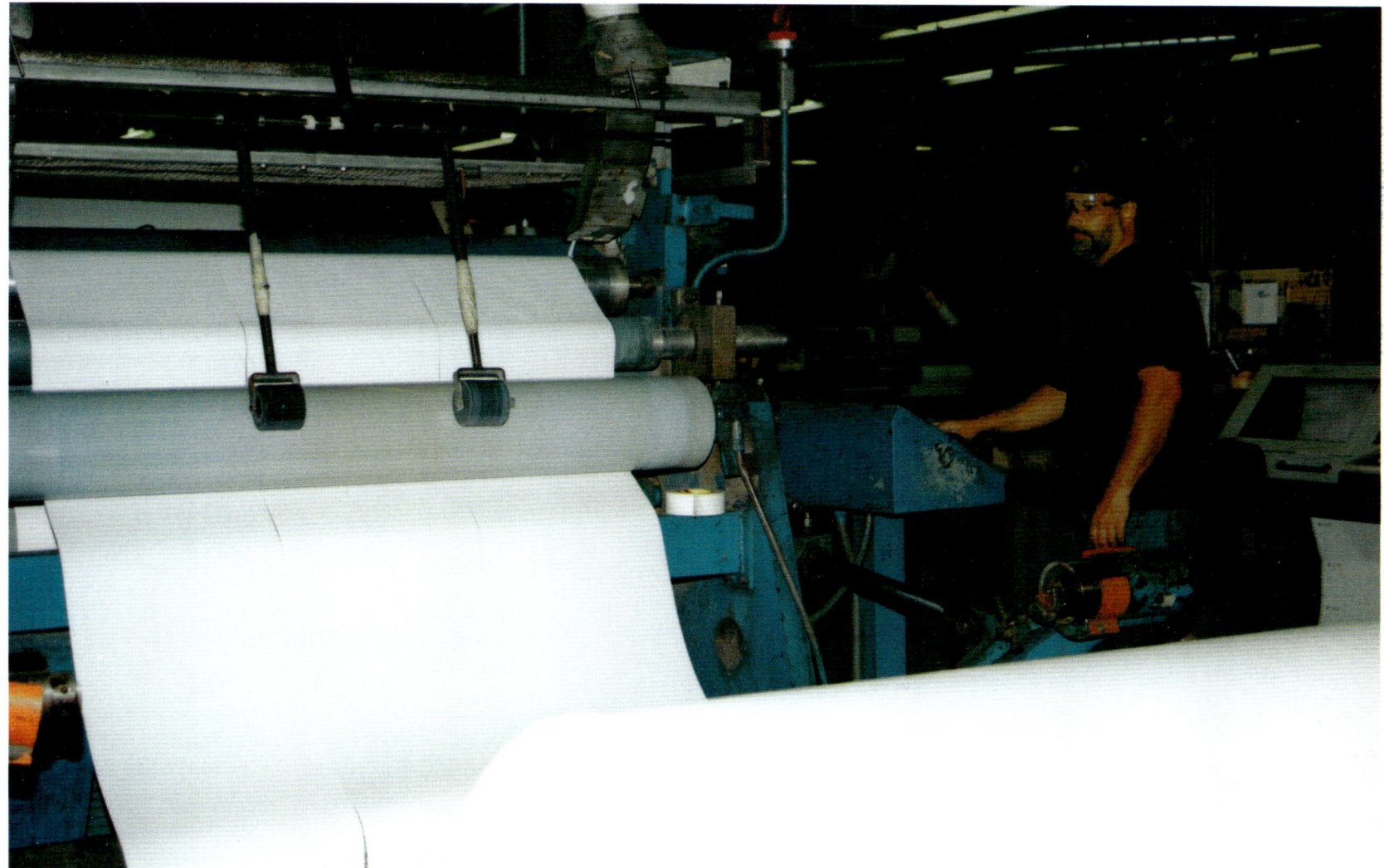

the plant, with a third press added in 1998, and a fourth in 2000. Clearly, Boise Cascade is here to stay.

And while it doesn't employ as many people as it did when it was a paper mill, Boise Cascade still runs two full shifts, and offers family wage jobs for the 79 employees now working at the plant. The smaller staff creates a tight-knit family of workers who feel they're part of a team. With a $4.4 million dollar payroll, the plant is growing all the time.

Boise Cascade continues its long tradition of contributing to the community. Boise donates paper products to schools and promotional items for charities to auction off. . . . All part of Boise Cascade's commitment to the community.

When Boise Cascade initially shut down its paper plant, some thought it would be the death of the company in Vancouver. But growth in the specialty security paper industry seems assured, and Vancouver Specialties is a profitable and productive business. In an industry that typically sees a lot of ups and downs, it's clear that the Boise Cascade team at Vancouver intends to grow and prosper.

Boise Cascade Corporation, headquartered in Boise, Idaho, is a major distributor of office products and building materials and an integrated manufacturer and distributor of paper and wood products.

Ordinary paper arrives at Vancouver Specialties and is converted into high-tech security paper destined to become checks, bank certificates, bonds, and other papers used in the banking industry.

The company owns and manages more than 2-million acres of timberland in the United States. A leader in sustainable forestry, Boise Cascade uses third-party audits and an advisory council of independent experts in its Forest Stewardship Program to ensure the protection of wildlife, plants, soil, and air and water quality. Visit the Boise Cascade Web site at www.bc.com.

WaferTech

DEDICATED TO MANUFACTURING ITS CUSTOMERS' CHIPS

Dedicated foundries are transforming the semiconductor industry.

In 1999, an estimated 10 percent of the integrated circuits (ICs) manufactured worldwide were produced by semiconductor foundries. According to market research firms, such as Dataquest and Semico Research, that figure is expected to soar to nearly 50 percent by the year 2010.

In the United States, there is only one dedicated semiconductor foundry—WaferTech, located on 260 acres in Camas, Washington.

Founded in June 1996, WaferTech was formed as a joint venture of Taiwan Semiconductor Manufacturing Company (TSMC); Altera Corp.; Analog Devices Inc.; and Integrated Silicon Solution Inc. TSMC, WaferTech's major owner-investor, is the creator and leader of the worldwide dedicated IC foundry industry.

Commercial production at WaferTech's state-of-the-art fabrication facility, or fab, got under way in mid-1998. Production output is approximately 20,000 wafers per month, and the company is progressing in its upward climb to at least 28,000 wafers per month by the end of the year 2000.

As a dedicated, or "pure play," foundry, WaferTech manufactures ICs to the specifications of its customers, while neither designing nor marketing chips under its own brand name. For customers, the outsourcing of IC manufacturing services has become increasingly attractive amid escalating costs of fab construction and maintaining advanced process technologies.

WaferTech's 1-million-square-foot fabrication complex is located on 260 acres in Camas, where high-tech growth has earned state attention.

The only dedicated semiconductor foundry in the nation, WaferTech provides advanced manufacturing services for customers with a diverse range of end-product applications.

Fabless companies—semiconductor companies that design and market ICs but do not own a fabrication facility—depend on dedicated foundries to make their products a reality. In recent years, the boom in communications, consumer electronics, computers, and other devices has caused this fabless segment to exceed the growth of the overall semiconductor market by nearly double. Meanwhile, more and more integrated device manufacturers, or IDMs—firms known for building products from top to bottom—are turning to foundries for highly sophisticated, made-to-order chips.

As global leader of the dedicated IC foundry industry, TSMC provides the most advanced process technology, library and IP options, and other leading-edge foundry services. WaferTech's fabrication processes are exact replications of TSMC's production-proven technology. Processes available from WaferTech include 0.35-micron mixed mode, 0.25-micron SRAM, 0.22-micron logic, and 0.18-micron logic, which was being transferred from TSMC to WaferTech in early 2000.

Continuing to improve technology and meet the demands of an ever-changing market would be challenge enough for most businesses. But as a startup, WaferTech has also worked hard to build employee unity and establish a company culture.

Just three years after its inception, WaferTech ranked within the top 10 largest private-sector employers in Clark County. By the end of the year 2000, the company's workforce is expected to swell to more than 1,250. WaferTech aims to flourish as a dedicated semiconductor foundry in the Silicon Forest.

Kyocera Industrial Ceramics Corporation

Kyocera Industrial Ceramics Corporation has its roots in Japan where it began as a manufacturer of ceramic insulators for television tubes. Today, Kyocera is an international company manufacturing a wide range of products, including semiconductor packages, electronic components, structural ceramics for industrial machines and engines, ceramic consumer products, such as knives and scissors, cellular and satellite telephones, laser printers, cameras, and photovoltaic solar cells.

A global network with more than 40 plants and 100 sales locations, Kyocera has a strong research and development component to create products that are original, innovative, and consumer oriented.

In 1990, Kyocera Industrial Ceramics Corporation (KICC) was founded in Vancouver, Washington, to develop and produce industrial and automotive ceramics. Its goal was, and continues to be, growing Kyocera's technical ceramics business.

Primarily a sales company selling the Kyocera products made in Japan, KICC also produces component ceramic parts that are used in gas turbine engines, heaters and ignitors for gas powered stoves and furnaces, fiber optics, and parts critical for the manufacture of semi-conductors.

Ceramics, while accepted as traditional technology in Japan, is still being "discovered" in America, giving KICC tremendous growth potential. The properties of ceramics, with its ability to tolerate extreme temperatures (2,500 degrees Fahrenheit), its low thermal expansion, and rigidity make it an ideal product for a variety of applications.

At KICC, slip casting, dry pressing, and injection molds are used to create the ceramic parts. High temperature pressure furnaces with nitrogen coating make the ceramics both strong and dense. Computer monitored grinding machines guarantee precision time and time again.

Diamond grinding is a specialty of KICC's products. Ceramic seals made for aircraft engines will have to rotate nearly 100,000 RPM, so they must be made to the highest specifications possible to withstand the heat and pressure.

Clients often come to KICC with the request to help design a ceramic part that was formerly created out of metal. Fortunately, KICC thrives on creative challenges.

Founder Kazuo Inamori had an attitude that continues to guide Kyocera today: "What we like to do next is what people tell us we can never do."

Kyocera's philosophy says it all: "Respect the divine and love people." An open style of management, an emphasis on teamwork, and a dedication to the community makes KICC a unique place to work. With an overriding policy of "do the right thing as a human being" Kyocera has developed a moral code that guides every aspect of the company's decisions.

On an international level, Kyocera and the Inamori Foundation sponsors the Kyoto prizes, awarded to individuals and groups which have made significant contributions to the advancement of society. On the local level, KICC generously shares its wealth with the Vancouver community.

KICC made a significant contribution to the low income health clinic Healthy Steps and towards the renovation of the home of Civil War hero O.O. Howard on Officers Row. YMCA, Identify Clark County and Leadership Clark County, and Celebrate Freedom are just some of the organizations that have benefited from KICC's desire to be a good citizen to the community.

Kyocera worldwide also sponsors a student exchange program where children of employees as well as children from community schools are sent to Japan for 10 days. Students from Japan are sent here at the same time. This program enforces Kyocera's cultural belief in global unity.

In a world where corporate profits are usually the number one objective, Kyocera has another point of view: To improve and heighten the souls of everyone with whom they connect. It's why Kyocera Industrial Ceramics Corporation is succeeding on so many levels.

(above left) Headquarters opened September 1992.
(below) Silicon Nitride gas turbine components.

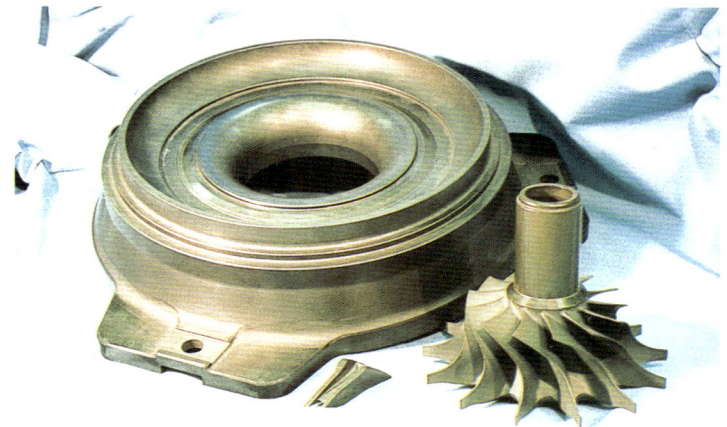

ConAgra Malt: Great Western Malting Company

Experience and consistency makes great malt which, in turn, creates great beer. The malt produced at the Great Western Malting Company in Vancouver has a worldwide reputation for excellence.

Great Western Malting Company employees.

Great Western is part of a global company known as ConAgra Malt. It was formed in 1996 as a joint-venture and quickly became one of the largest malt producers in the world, gaining 11 percent of the world's malt production.

With operating plants in the United States, Canada, the United Kingdom, Australia, and China, ConAgra Malt has a total production capacity of 1,302,000 metric tons. Some of the world's largest brewers trust their beer production to the malt produced by ConAgra, including Anheuser-Busch, Heineken, Kirin, Labatt, Molson, Fosters, and Asahi.

The Great Western Malting Company consists of three U.S. operations in Vancouver, Washington; Pocatello, Idaho; and Los Angeles, California; with global headquarters in Vancouver. The three locations give the company advantageous distribution channels. Great Western has been producing a range of malt for brewers in the western United States, Latin America, and Pacific rim countries since 1934, with a total capacity of 320,000 metric tons.

Great Western uses two-row and six-row barley from Idaho and eastern Washington, as well as parts of Montana and southern Oregon. Quality control is a priority; all grain is double checked when it first arrives by rail at the facility and samples are immediately sent to a lab for analysis.

The Vancouver facility not only has modern Saladin-style compartment houses for producing malt, but also the original drum-style system. These drums were built in 1934, right after the repeal of prohibition, to meet the needs of Northwest breweries. Each batch of grain averages 238,000 pounds, and utilizes a pneumatic system to pull the air through the drums for germination.

The demand for specialized micro-brews has meant a need for specialty malt, and Vancouver is answering that call. In 1998, a new roast-house was constructed, along with a truck-loading facility, giving the company the ability to create custom malts for micro-brewery clients. Great Western is a leader in the industry for micro-brewery malt, producing a wide range of malt for ale, lager, wheat, porter, and stout beers.

Great Western is proud to have been a stable employer in the community for years, offering jobs for local residents. Employment at Great Western is often a family affair, and many employees put in 35 to 40 years of service by retirement. The company views the workforce as one of its competitive advantages; employees work hard and contribute ideas for enhancing the partnerships with key customers. Great Western also prides itself on being a good corporate citizen and a good steward of the environment, with strict compliance to environmental rules and regulations.

From the steeping to the germination to the kilning, Great Western uses modern techniques plus age-old knowledge and instinct to develop great malts. Creating malt is as much art as it is science; it is a formula that Great Western has perfected.

Ronnie Jernagan receives "Safe Worker of the Year-1999" award from President/CEO Gary Mize.

Photo by Cliff Barbour

A Portrait of Prosperity

The Business Community

Chapter 11

Greater Vancouver Chamber of Commerce, 120

Columbia Credit Union, 122

LSW Architects, P.C., 124

West Coast Bank, 126

Design Showroom, Inc., 127

Lacamas Community Credit Union, 128

Clark County School Employees Credit Union, 129

Photos by Cliff Barbour

Greater Vancouver Chamber of Commerce

(above) *The Marshall House, one of many historic homes saved along Officers Row, was once the home for General George C. Marshall while he was an officer stationed at Vancouver Barracks.*

If it's important to business in Clark County, it's important to the Greater Vancouver Chamber of Commerce. That's why the Chamber has been the voice of business for Southwest Washington since 1890.

The Chamber is a voluntary alliance of businesses, professionals, and organizations. Working together, Chamber members take an active stance on issues that uphold sound principles and practices for business. United, they continue to raise the bar on the quality of life enjoyed by the community.

The Greater Vancouver Chamber is the largest, strongest, and most active business organization in Southwest Washington. Always seeking ways to add value for members, the Chamber provides an array of services including advocacy, business resources, and networking events. The Chamber serves its members by being responsive to their needs.

Whether it's consulting on the revitalization of downtown Vancouver or the construction of state roads, the Greater Vancouver Chamber of Commerce is active in public affairs. As the community recognizes the need to attract industry to the area to increase the economic base, so has the Chamber grown and changed to respond to those needs.

Today, the Chamber is the business organization in Clark County with the strongest perspective on public policy issues. Part of the role of advocate includes educating the community at large about business issues. Each year, the public affairs division of the Chamber partners or leads educational forums that are open to members and the public.

The Greater Vancouver Chamber of Commerce, based on national chamber standards, has reached the top level of sophistication of services provided. At this level, its focus is to nurture partnerships, strengthen coalitions, and continue to be the regional voice of business in both political and legislative arenas.

The Chamber is always looking for new ways to help its members, whether big or small, with tangible resources. On a regular basis the Chamber makes referrals to member businesses for services or products they offer. The Chamber staff also acts as an informational referral source, fielding over 20,000 questions on behalf of the Clark County business community and distributing thousands of publications in response to information requests.

The Chamber has recently welcomed the Service Corps of Retired Executives (SCORE) organization into its building. This partnership allows new start-up businesses, or struggling

(below) *A young boy and dog enjoy playtime at a local neighborhood park. Parks, greenspace, public gardens, and youth facilities are high priorities for the community.*

businesses, an opportunity to receive free one-on-one business counseling from experienced volunteers.

Another resource for Chamber members is the Affinity programs. These programs are exclusive partnerships between the Chamber and member businesses, offering better rates on services or products for Chamber members. There is a growing menu of Affinity programs that meet strict criteria for providing value to members.

As is true with all Chambers, members have the opportunity to gain wider name recognition in the business community by sponsoring a Chamber event or product. These sponsorships, in addition to other advertising opportunities, are a resource for members looking for a cost-effective means to market their business.

On a regular basis the Chamber sponsors training seminars to provide skills for individuals or organizations. Popular seminar topics include how to network effectively, marketing to improve company image, and making effective group presentations.

Members who participate in Chamber networking activities quickly find the niche areas that benefit their business. There is an abundance of networking opportunities targeting different needs, audiences, formats, and times of day so that every Chamber member will find an event of value to them. Often, a Chamber member's first networking opportunity occurs at orientation where they learn the benefits of Chamber membership.

There are two main categories for Chamber networking events: monthly and annual. The monthly events offer members opportunities to meet new business prospects and promote their business. By attending these events regularly, members gain valuable name recognition and form long-lasting business relationships. The annual events are produced on a grand scale and attract a much larger audience. Pairing many of the annual events with a business trade show is an opportunity for members to display their products or explain their services in more depth.

While the Chamber is the voice of the business community, it also seeks to be a good community partner and lends its support to broad community issues. The Chamber is guided by six core values: leadership, membership services, advocacy, participation, collaboration, and accountability. These six values are measured against every potential program, service, or public-policy issue.

The Chamber has a long history of initiating partnerships to fulfill community needs. Most recently, the Chamber launched a school-to-work program collaborating with the local K-12 school district, community college, and university. The Chamber also played a role in creating a new Visitor and Convention Bureau. With multiple partners the Chamber facilitated the development of the Lewis and Clark Bicentennial Commemorative Committee to spearhead efforts that will begin locally in 2003.

(above) Vancouver was the original site for the Hudson Bay Trading Company, lending its heritage to the many layers of history that are found within the Vancouver National Historic Reserve.

(below) Esther Short Park is the crown jewel in the center of downtown Vancouver. At the park, Vancouverites enjoy the start of their Farmer's Market in the spring, summer concerts, and art festivals in the fall.

Both the high-technology industries and local neighborhood associations have formally aligned with the Chamber to form Councils that address needs of interest to those groups. Obviously, the wide range of appeal for other organizations to partner with the Chamber illustrates its leadership role in the community.

The Greater Vancouver Chamber of Commerce is closely associated with two other organizations in an affiliate relationship. Although both Community Choices 2010 and Leadership Clark County have stand-alone boards of directors, programs, and staff, these programs benefit from this affiliation by receiving increased visibility, access to the business community, and public relations.

Community Choices 2010's mission is to support strategies that lead Clark County to a brighter future in three vital areas: education, health and safety, and violence prevention. Community Choices 2010 set benchmarks for the community's health and publishes a report card documenting the successes and challenges in reaching those benchmarks.

Leadership Clark County is a nine-month training program for tomorrow's leaders. With exposure to community issues such as economic development, education, health care, justice, and others, participants gain valuable resources, learn new skills, and become part of the solution to these issues. Formed in 1994, Leadership Clark County now boasts of alumni on boards, commissions, and neighborhood associations making a positive difference in the community.

A look through the list of Chamber members will show some long-standing businesses that have been members for literally decades, a few for over a century. This loyalty and longevity is a clear sign that the Greater Vancouver Chamber of Commerce not only seeks, but delivers prosperity for its members and community.

Led by a volunteer board of the most respected business individuals in the community, the Chamber will continue to move forward with a vision creating a future that balances the benefits of economic vitality and quality of life expected by the people who live and work in the Clark County community.

Columbia Credit Union

SERVING CLARK COUNTY AND HAYDEN ISLAND/JANTZEN BEACH

Columbia Credit Union has a strong history beginning in Clark County in 1952. Now, Columbia is one of the largest credit unions in the metropolitan area with over 53,000 members and assets in excess of $356 million. Approximately 200 employees serve their member-owners in nine (soon to be 10) Clark County offices. Plus, Columbia owns ATMs in several community hubs including Jantzen Beach Carousel, Jantzen Beach DoubleTree, Red Lion at the Quay, Clark County Courthouse, Southwest Washington Medical Center, Veterans Administration Hospital, City Center Cinemas, and Washington State University at Vancouver. To meet its community's needs Columbia provides ATM access at events such as the Home & Garden Idea Fair and the Clark County Fair.

SATISFIED MEMBERSHIP

Columbia's President and CEO David Doss summarized member satisfaction saying, "We're proud of our 16 consecutive awards for Five-Star Superior financial performance. I believe many of our member-owners prefer Columbia because of our service quality, product choice, and ease of access, and because of our fiscal soundness we're able to continually improve in all these areas." Laurie Kusch, who joined Columbia in 1975 and serves as vice president quality service management, adds, "Our members really notice our service quality. When reviewing our member surveys it's not the services we offer, but how we offer them that is mentioned so frequently."

A volunteer Board of Directors makes decisions locally, and profits return to members via better loan rates or higher deposit rates. Members are shareholders in the credit union, which is why they call the annual report the "Annual Owners Report" and the quarterly newsletter is aptly named, "The Owners Manual." Dixie Shaw, senior vice president marketing and business development, commented on Columbia's commitment to its member-owners by saying, "The quality of our products and services are reflected in our member feedback surveys which show a 90 percent plus satisfaction level." Shaw continues, "Between service shoppers, a commitment to staff training and staff incentive plans, our employees are extremely vigilant towards providing excellent member service. Members expect only the best from Columbia!"

NUMBER ONE FINANCIAL INSTITUTION

Columbia received the number one Financial Institution rating from the *Columbian Newspaper's* "Best of Clark County Readership Poll" and the same number one rating in the 2000 TOMA Institute's Survey, which measures unaided recall and market share. Why do people think of Columbia as the number one Financial Institution in Clark County? Dee Anne Cloke, Columbia's vice president human resource, explains, "Happy employees are the root of our success. Our recent *Washington CEO Magazine's* 'Best Company to Work For' award proves that our employees think highly of our corporate culture. This attitude provides our members with better service." Cloke continues, "Considering the number of Clark County banking choices, we rely on our friendly professional staff to outshine our competitors and solidify our members' loyalty. This is done with great teamwork—and that only happens when employees are willing to go the extra mile. Not just for the member, but for their co-workers too."

Columbia works hard for its member-owners. Pictured here, the management team enjoys an off-site team-building event—where they obviously play hard too!

THE NATURAL CHOICE

Recently, Columbia renovated its core line of deposit accounts. Listening to its member-owners was the catalyst to many of its account changes and improvements. From adding a complete department that meets business service requests to product specific changes, such as revamping the 50-plus senior checking Rewards PLUS club account, Columbia is serious about not resting on its laurels. After surveying its club members, Columbia discovered that discounts to local events and restaurants would be a popular benefit for Rewards PLUS club members. With this in mind, Columbia quickly struck a deal with Entertainment Books, Inc. adding them as a new feature for club members who also use Columbia's tiered money-market account. It's Columbia's commitment to listening to its member-owners' needs, looking for the best solutions, and then acting in the members' best interest that differentiates Columbia's products and services from local competitors.

To build community awareness, Columbia advertises in local newspapers, on television, theater screens, and billboards.

Moreover, personal visits to local businesses extend Columbia Credit Union's personal touch. Columbia also tells its story through a leading edge digital business card. The digital business card is a mini-CD that provides an entertaining six-minute infomercial of Columbia's products and services. The digital business card offers a link to Columbia's Website www.columbiacu.org for current rates and information. Columbia proactively assesses Clark County residents' future needs while letting them know how Columbia can help them benefit financially today.

Columbia's digital business card looks like a traditional business card but functions like a multi-media tool.

BUSINESS SERVICES AND MORTGAGES

"When our business-owning members said they had to do their business banking elsewhere, we listened, and we acted," states Chuck Anderson, Columbia's vice president commercial and real estate lending. Now, businesses regularly call on Columbia regarding dividend-paying business checking accounts, merchant services, business Visas, and a variety of business loan options. Columbia has a full-service business department that delivers what businesses want and need. Anderson adds, "Our Real Estate Lending Department is also known for its sophistication in meeting member needs." Bart Wescom, Columbia's assistant vice president real estate lending, recently garnered Columbia an "Employer of the Year" award from the Association of Professional Mortgage Women. Columbia provides a complete line of traditional, non-conforming, construction, equity, and government-backed mortgage options.

INVOLVED

Columbia Credit Union is one of Clark County's major corporate community event sponsors and over 70 percent of its staff volunteers. A short list of Columbia's involvement includes: The Clark County Fair, Neighborhood Backyard Concerts, Taste of Vancouver, American Cancer Society's 24-Hour Relay for Life, March of Dimes, American Red Cross, and Southwest Washington Medical Center Foundation efforts. Columbia is represented on many other community and service organization boards including: Leadership Clark County (LCC), Clark County Skills Center, Columbia River Economic Development Council (CREDC), Identity Clark County (ICC), Vancouver's Downtown Association (VDA), Community Housing Resource Center, Evergreen Habitat for Humanity, and Southwest Washington Independent Forward Thrust (SWIFT).

EASE OF ACCESS

Columbia offers access through the Internet, telephone, and personal contact through community outreach. And, with nine Clark County branches, Columbia isn't overlooking traditional methods of expansion and member access. Paul Hodge, Columbia's chief operating officer and senior vice president, adds, "We just settled into our Battle Ground at Fred Meyer location and we relocated our Orchards branch to the Albertson's/Home Base complex. Now, we're negotiating for a new location in east Clark County." Branches offer drive-up, ATM, and in-lobby service areas. The newest offices feature lobby self-serve coin counters, computer terminals, and automated cash dispensers.

Columbia Credit Union meets and exceeds the needs of even the most discriminating Clark County Resident. It is a member-owned financial cooperative that not only supports the community, but it also provides members with the deposit and loan services they need throughout their life. The highly acclaimed Columbia Credit Union is the financial institution of choice—the natural choice!

Columbia Credit Union celebrates with Battle Ground Fred Meyer during Columbia's first in-store branch Grand Opening. Pictured from left: CCU Board Chair Mark Ail, CCU Sr. VP/COO Paul Hodge, Fred Meyer Store Director Jim Harvey, and CCU President/CEO David Doss.

LSW Architects, P.C.

A fresh commitment to traditional values and a new twist on client involvement set LSW Architects apart from the rest of the field.

Founded as a sole-proprietorship in 1955, this architectural, planning, and interior design firm now extends its influence well beyond the walls of its original Clark County home. Now occupying offices in both Vancouver, Washington, and Portland, Oregon, its staff of 38 is able to successfully serve clients throughout the region. Continuing to focus primarily on public works, LSW has expanded its portfolio to include some 700 such projects. Noted recent examples of its work include: Skyview High School, Heritage High School, Stoller Middle School, Vancouver YMCA, Propstra Community Center, Washington State Department of Licensing building, and Discovery Middle School. Recent revitalization and modernization efforts include Hudson's Bay High School, Hough Elementary School, and Fort Vancouver High School.

LSW's design works and innovative solutions consistently garner national recognition for the firm: exemplified by the many top awards its projects have earned. What really sets LSW apart, however, actually has less to do with its design ability than it does with the process it has developed to really "engage" the client. With most of LSW's clients, this means enhanced community involvement.

Developing an initial "ground-swell" of support, maintaining positive "energy" throughout the project, tapping all creative resources, and ultimately assuring project satisfaction are all LSW project goals. The community's desire for increased involvement in the design phases would normally be considered a complication to this process: possibly even a real burden to the schedule. With a desire to instill real "ownership" in the solution, however, LSW recognized a rich resource in the community itself, saw their desire as an asset, and sought a way to create a "win-win" situation for all involved.

Motivated by a need to reform the traditional programming/conceptual design phase of school design and through collaborative effort with a most visionary and forward-thinking school district a unique and particularly intense two-day, project kick-off session was devised. With "partner" Vancouver Schools, this approach was initially employed on Vancouver's Discovery Middle School project. This "symposium" process has now been used on more than 40 subsequent works and has, in fact, become a mainstay of LSW's planning arsenal.

As stated, the process is "intense": a serious understatement at times. Sixty to 100 parents, students, administrators, staff, legislators, planners, and LSW's own design key team members are brought together into this 48-hour, multi-faceted idea-generating, and concept-producing session. Designers have to be able to genuinely listen, to work without inhibition/ego, must "magically" capture the essence of the workshop, and must quickly present the results with excitement and flair.

(above left) Skyview High School, Vancouver, WA

(below) Heritage High School, Vancouver, WA

Three distinct concepts are generally produced: allowing subsequent design efforts to focus on a "hybrid" of the best ideas. The hybrid then represents the best of what the community or client was saying and is truly "owned" by the participants.

The measure of "project success" is ofttimes difficult to ascertain and even then, it may be years in realization. The success in these "symposium" projects is sensed immediately, however. Tangible evidence that LSW really "listened" abound throughout. The schedule has been met and the budget maintained. There is great pride of ownership in the design, and those who took part in the process know they were heard because they see the results before them.

Nationally, much attention has been focused on LSW's public works and on this true, hands-on community involvement process. As an example, Vancouver's Discovery Middle School was awarded the top award from six national architectural and educational organizations. The process itself earned LSW a role on the White House Millennium Council on Education, which works with Secretary of Education Riley to seek solutions to the "school as community center." Districts are increasingly turning to LSW for assistance with their pre-bond efforts also: drawing from LSW's multiple expertise.

Aside from the success that can be attributed, LSW and the owners who engage in this virtual "hands-on" process, truly enjoy the experience and look forward to participation. Being first and foremost a client-driven architectural and planning firm, this process elaboration greatly augments its already established commitment of service.

Its application now coincides with LSW's planning efforts in retail and commercial project types as well. Such Clark County successes include the Propstra Community Center, the Vancouver YMCA, the Department of Licensing building, Hillcrest Church, Branches Bookstore, and various other commercial works. Developers and builders alike know that their needs will be attended to with the highest priority dispatch and the greatest care and that documents will be complete, timely, and considerate of their own particular construction requirements.

Teamwork established in initial projects generally leads to long-term relationships. The staff of LSW creates its own "mission statement" for a project: drawn from the goals and needs of that client. Staff members extend the resources of the firm and their own personal energies well beyond mere "adequate" professional care: greatly exceeding expectations and contributing very real added value to the project.

(above) Skyview High School Auditorium

(below) Sherwood YMCA, Sherwood, Oregon

Led by four principals, Vaughn Lein, Arlen Stanek, Ralph Willson, and John Wyckoff, and six associates, LSW is ushering in the 21st century with great energy and high expectations: for itself as well as for its "partners" in the community.

West Coast Bank

In a time when less and less service seems to be the status quo of the banking industry, one bank stands out as dedicated to providing quality service. In fact, it's one of the trademarks of West Coast Bank: Service is Our Signature.

Lisa Dow, West Coast Bank credit administrator, with customer Mark Sonney, Yard 'N Garden Land.

West Coast Bank is a new name, but the company has a long history in the Pacific Northwest, dating back to 1925. As the 21st century neared, it consolidated affiliate banks including Bank of Vancouver to become West Coast Bank.

Mergers can sometimes lead to frustration and fewer services for bank customers. That wasn't the case at West Coast Bank, because the bank held onto its core values of integrity, exceptional customer service, and local decision making. That's what continues to make West Coast Bank a superior place for all banking services.

With 40 branches in both Washington and Oregon, and $1.3 billion in assets, West Coast Bank is large enough to meet the needs of individuals as well as small and mid-sized businesses. But because it is local and not run by some huge corporation back east, it is fully engaged in the community with highly trained employees who work to tailor their products to each customer.

There's no "cookie-cutter" list of criteria for loans, because West Coast Bank prides itself on being community and customer focused. That's why, while other banks said "no," West Coast Bank invested in projects such as a local recreation center and helped a local farmer with a development business opportunity.

West Coast Bank is a full financial services company, with an active trust and investment presence in the Vancouver area. This enables West Coast Bank to help a client with trust and estate planning, to recommend someone to help draw up a will, buy and sell securities, set up annuities, and even find life or disability insurance.

West Coast Bank is a blend of old-fashioned values and high-tech services. It has plenty of ATMs to serve its customers, and on-line banking for the techno-savvy, but there is never a lack of tellers in the branch offices ready to give one-on-one service. That's because West Coast Bank hasn't forgotten that a lot of its customers would rather deal with a person than a machine.

At West Coast Bank, tellers know their customers by name, and vice versa. Bank employees live in the community, and take part in such organizations as Rotary and the Vancouver Chamber of Commerce.

Exceptional service extends to West Coast Bank business clients, too. It offers on-line banking service for payroll, deposits, and bill payment. West Coast Bank representatives routinely show up at local businesses, just to see how things are going and discuss how they can make any improvements. The bank also provides courier services to help companies make their deposits more easily.

All the services of a big banking corporation, but with an important "extra"—personalized, old-fashioned service. That's why West Coast Bank is truly the alternative to the mass-market banking seen elsewhere, and why service will always be the number-one priority.

Dennis Hall, left, West Coast Bank branch manager, with customers Vinton and Helen Erickson, Erickson Farm Market.

Design Showroom, Inc.

Many interior designers have come and gone in the past decade, but during the same time, Design Showroom, Inc. has grown and thrived. The reason? The people of Design Showroom, Inc. make customer service their number one priority.

Husband and wife team Don and Marlene Brown began an interior design and planning company in 1984. One year later, Terry Murphy joined them. By the early '90s, Don was bowing out and Terry and Marlene formed Design Showroom, Inc., a woman-owned and operated company dedicated to providing the best in interior design.

Located in the heart of downtown Vancouver, Design Showroom has a team of dedicated, enthusiastic, and experienced women who use their talents to design perfect settings for their clients. Whether it be a new home, a remodel project, or a commercial project, Design Showroom has the innovative and creative answer.

Never afraid of a challenge, Terry Murphy and Marlene Brown have taken on design projects for such businesses as Riverview Community Bank, Heritage Place Condominiums in downtown Vancouver, and local executive homes.

Their success comes from not only hard work, but also from customer satisfaction. In all its years of operation, Design Showroom has never needed to use conventional advertising. Word of mouth alone has built the business to more than a million dollars annually.

It comes down to chemistry and intuition. Murphy and Brown know that they can't be all things to all people. So they rely on their experience and a "gut" feeling when taking on projects. They want to make sure a job is a good fit for everyone concerned. And they would rather see a client go elsewhere than to take on a job they know doesn't suit them.

It is a philosophy that has served them well. They don't just end up with satisfied clients, but with friends and relationships that continue to bring more referrals.

Developing relationships with their clients is a key to Design Showroom's success. But so is thoughtful and careful use of the client's money. The standard is simple: Design Showroom spends every cent of the client's money as if it were its own.

Design Showroom, Inc. has a solid team of sub-contractors behind it to bring its creative ideas to life. Many of the contractors have been working for Design Showroom, Inc. for years, some of them exclusively.

Murphy and Brown are passionate about what they do. They're also passionate about the town in which they do it. Design Showroom, Inc. is a member of the Vancouver Chamber of Commerce. The company has donated bedding, towels, and other items for YWCA transition homes.

Terry Murphy serves on "Identity Clark County" to promote the revitalization of downtown Vancouver and is a strong supporter of the YWCA. Marlene Brown has lived in Vancouver since she was 12 years old and is active with Boy and Girl Scouts. They know it's their privilege and responsibility to give back to the community.

It's a community that's growing rapidly. And Design Showroom, Inc. is there to help it look great.

(above left) Owners Terry Murphy and Marlene Brown.

(below) Design Showroom's conference room.

Lacamas Community Credit Union

Anyone who lives or works in Camas, Vancouver, or Washougal is eligible to join the 15,000 satisfied members of the Lacamas Community Credit Union. Unlike other credit unions that require members to belong to a specific profession, Lacamas exists to serve all of its neighbors.

Lacamas Credit Union is a not-for-profit financial institution owned entirely by its members and operated exclusively for their benefit. Since it operates on a not-for-profit basis, earnings are returned to members in the form of lower rates on loans, higher rates on deposits, fewer fees and charges, and an investment in knowledgeable, friendly staff.

Its stability and strong financial position allows the credit union to offer the same variety of services as any mega-bank: auto, home, student, or personal loans; federally insured investment options for either short or long term; credit lines; and of course, personal checking, including free checking, business checking, and its famous senior checking.

Lacamas also has all the high-tech services customers demand in today's busy world. Members can go on line 24 hours a day to check account balances, transfer funds, pay bills, get copies of cleared checks, order checks, open new accounts—even apply for a loan!

With five branches—two in Vancouver, one in Washougal, and two in Camas—members have plenty of options for personal attention to

their banking needs, no matter where they live. And Lacamas Credit Union has formed an alliance with other credit unions, giving members access to over 4,000 surcharge-free ATMs nationwide including over 30 in Clark County.

But what sets Lacamas Credit Union apart from other banking institutions is the commitment to the community it serves. Many members live in homes that were financed by Lacamas, and much of the recent growth in the region is directly due to the reinvestments made by Lacamas. Both the credit union and the community have "grown up" together, and after more than 65 years of service, Lacamas understands how it can best serve its members.

Lacamas Credit Union doesn't just want to meet its members needs, it wants to exceed them. Members can always talk to a real person at the credit union to get fast resolution to any problems. When reviewing a loan application, Lacamas doesn't try to see how much money it can make off of a person, but what will truly be the best option for each specific member.

Lacamas takes that commitment to service out into the community, as well. It offers college scholarships to local high school graduates and supports charities and events such as Doernbecher Children's Hospital, Junior Achievement, and the Clark County Fair. Employees even give "hands-on" attention to building floats for the annual Camas Days parade.

At Lacamas, "member owned" isn't just lip service; it's a way of doing business. Lacamas Credit Union makes every decision with one question behind it: "How will this affect our members?" Lacamas wants to make sure every aspect of its business will ensure maximum value for members.

A solid financial institution with a long tradition of personal service. Membership that's open to anyone in the region. Lacamas Community Credit Union is here for you.

(top) Camas 5th Avenue Branch with drive-up ATM.

(left) Cascade Park Branch located on Chkalov Drive in Vancouver.

Clark County School Employees Credit Union

For more than 60 years, Clark County School Employees Credit Union has existed for one reason: Providing the very best financial service to its members.

"Education, in all its many forms, is a life-long commitment—and a commitment that shows in everything we do." Roger Michaelis, President/CEO

A HISTORY OF CARING.

During the Great Depression of the 1930s, a small group of Vancouver schoolteachers pooled their savings so that other educators could obtain an unsecured, low-interest loan. That simple act of kindness laid the foundation for what would become Clark County School Employees Credit Union.

Formed by and for teachers, the founders gradually expanded their membership base. Within the past few years, the field of membership has opened further, allowing anyone who lives or works in Southwest Washington to join.

As a "financial cooperative" that is locally owned and operated, the Credit Union is still governed as it was 60 years ago—by a volunteer Board of Directors. The Credit Union's goals today are the same as they have always been: Delivering financial services that exceed member expectations.

PUTTING EDUCATION FIRST.

As a champion of education, Clark County School Employees Credit Union believes that learning is something that is never outgrown. "For us," says President and CEO Roger Michaelis, "Education, in all its many forms, is a life-long commitment—and a commitment that shows in everything we do."

To start grade school students on the road to literacy, the Credit Union sponsors "Read With Me"—a unique program that gives area school children free books.

To give high school students a true "hands-on" learning experience, the Credit Union oversees a trio of fully operational campus branches in local high schools. While students learn the process and procedure of doing financial transactions for a credit union, they also learn the life-lessons of communication, teamwork, and planning.

To help local high school students, college students, and educators achieve their education goals, six different $1,000 scholarships are offered each year.

And to benefit all members, seminars are provided throughout the year on topics ranging from home ownership and auto loans to insurance options, saving for retirement, and estate planning.

MAKING THE CONNECTION.

Clark County School Employees Credit Union offers a variety of time-saving services to help members make the most of their valuable time. The Anytime Loan program gives members the freedom to apply for a loan over the Internet (www.ccsecu.com) or phone, instead of coming into a branch. Desktop Computer Branch℠ lets members review their accounts on line—day or night, using any personal computer. Desktop Computer Branch℠ Desktop Bill Payer℠ service allows members to pay their monthly bills electronically, without writing checks. And a network of fee-free ATMs lets members get cash on the go.

Service at the Credit Union means a friendly face, a knowledgeable answer, and the tools to help members make the most of their hard-earned money. Though times have changed and technologies have evolved, what made Clark County School Employees Credit Union strong in 1940 is the same thing that keeps it strong today. Members.

So what's in store for the next 60 years? Innovative technologies that help members save time and money. Financial services that exceed member expectations. And the best possible standard of service.

Through innovative on-line programs, members can review account balances, apply for loans, pay bills, and more—all electronically, from home or work.

A Portrait of Prosperity

Real Estate, Development, & Construction

Chapter 12

Norris, Beggs & Simpson, 132

Century 21 Complete Realty, 133

Tapani Underground, 134

North Coast Electric Company, 135

Otak and Killian Pacific, 136

Photos by Cliff Barbour

Norris, Beggs & Simpson

Vancouver is definitely a real estate "hot spot" right now, and NB&S has a depth of knowledge and understanding of that market to help its clients meet their needs. Norris, Beggs & Simpson's integrity and credibility has built a thriving business in Vancouver based on the understanding that it succeeds when its clients succeed.

Currently in its management portfolio, NB&S helped Electric Lightwave, Inc., with its Site Selection as well as consulting on the project through completion and move in.

Clark County has seen phenomenal growth in the past few years, with families and businesses alike moving to this corner of the Pacific Northwest. Finding the right location in which a business can settle can be difficult, unless a firm has the help of a professional real estate source such as Norris, Beggs & Simpson.

Whatever a firm's real estate needs, Norris, Beggs & Simpson offers it—brokerage services, mortgage banking, asset/property management, and even unique support services such as market research and analysis.

With offices in both Vancouver, Washington, and Portland, Oregon, as well as Bellevue, Washington, NB&S has employees with years of knowledge and experience in the different disciplines of commercial real estate. Using a "team" approach to maximize their knowledge and tailor it to a client's unique needs, NB&S serves buyers, sellers, lessors, lessees, developers, and investors.

NB&S was founded in 1932 in Portland, Oregon, by A. D. Norris, George J. Beggs, David Simpson, and Phillip D. Miller. At the beginning, they were merely property managers, but quickly expanded their services into mortgage lending and commercial and industrial brokerage.

While always offering service into the Vancouver area, in 1985, NB&S opened an office there for its customer's convenience. With five brokers, a manager, two property managers, and support staff, it's definitely not just a satellite office. Nor do the employees think of it as an offshoot of Portland. All of the employees who work in the Vancouver office also live in the community; they raise their families, pay taxes, and have a commitment to the success of the area.

NB&S has extensive background in office, industrial land, and retail property. Its expertise in the Vancouver region helped attract such companies as Kyocera Ceramics, Tektronix, Hewlett-Packard, and other high-tech firms to the county. NB&S can proudly take a lot of credit for the business growth out to 164th Avenue. Its thumbprints can also be seen in all of the major development areas from Fisher's Landing to Mill Plain, the mall area, and now moving north up Interstate 5.

Sometimes, though, a client doesn't fit the typical fee or transaction possibilities. In those cases, NB&S can do an extensive analysis of a company's specific needs, to help it decide if buying, leasing, or even a build-to-suit is the best option. Many clients have benefited from this special service of NB&S.

Its interest in the future of Clark County is just one reason NB&S hosts an annual real estate forecast breakfast in Vancouver. It gives CEOs, community leaders, and developers the chance to get an overview of the real estate market for the coming year. This free event requires extensive preparation by NB&S employees to make sure they have the best and most up-to-date statistics, but they see it as one more contribution to the community.

The breakfast not only lets NB&S show off its expertise and depth of market knowledge, but gives the community a chance to get real estate data and demographics that focus exclusively on the Vancouver area, something rarely found.

Years of experience and knowledge has taught NB&S that every relationship it forms is for the "long term." And it expects to continue that long-term relationship with Clark County for years to come.

NB&S played a key role in the development of McGillvray Place, owned by McGillvray Place Associates, LLC. Besides development consulting, NB&S handled initial lease up and continues to handle leasing for the project.

Century 21 Complete Realty

Buying or selling a home is a big step, but it doesn't have to be a misstep when CENTURY 21 Complete Realty is the real estate company. All CENTURY 21 offices are independently owned and operated, but the CENTURY 21 office at 416 NE 112th in Vancouver is also award winning and staffed by realtors who are experienced professionals dedicated to complete customer service and satisfaction.

CENTURY 21 Complete Realty is locally owned and operated by Sara Baird. The company also employs a full-time office manager. Both realtors and clients are invited to take advantage of Sara's open door policy. If there are any questions or concerns, CENTURY 21 Complete Realty is structured to answer the questions and address any and all concerns promptly.

This company has been the number one CENTURY 21 office in Southwest Washington since it opened its doors in 1988.

CENTURY 21 Complete Realty has earned the corporate quality service award more than any other CENTURY 21 office in the area. It has also earned the coveted Centurion Award, given to offices that achieve a million dollars in gross closed commissions.

Customer service is key to the company's philosophy and continued success. Its realtors know that educating their clients on the ins and outs of the real estate process, whether a buyer or a seller, is paramount to a successful transaction and satisfied customers. In this way, clients become better able to make clear decisions about what probably is the most important financial step they'll ever take in their life.

"Whatever it takes to make the client happy" is the motto at CENTURY 21 Complete Realty. From finding a mortgage company for a new buyer, to helping set up a garage sale for a seller, nobody ever says, "that's not my job." Realtors roll up their sleeves and dig in to do what's needed to make the purchase or sale a success for all concerned.

CENTURY 21 Complete Realty stresses continuing education for its realtors. The office has its own real estate school both for training new realtors and providing on-going education for established realtors. While the state of Washington requires a minimum number of hours of education, CENTURY 21 Complete Realty's educational standard is double that of the state. Knowing just the basic laws isn't enough for CENTURY 21 Complete.

Every CENTURY 21 Complete Realty client receives a written guarantee insuring quality service, including clearly stated objectives. The client knows from the start that their realtor will offer professional counsel, strong negotiation, full disclosure, and constant communication.

CENTURY 21 is an internationally known company—the largest real estate franchise in the world. But it's the personal attention and professional dedication given by each realtor at CENTURY 21 Complete that is responsible for the continued overall success of this office . . . one satisfied client at a time.

Tapani Underground

Any building or road has to have a firm foundation, or it will fail. Any business needs a firm foundation, as well, or it won't succeed. Tapani Underground is a construction company with a solid foundation of family integrity that specializes in making good foundations for construction projects.

Started in 1983 by Iner Tapani with a $3,000-dollar loan from his parents, Tapani Underground prepares sites for commercial and industrial buildings and road preparation.

Tapani Underground is more than just a trustworthy construction firm, it is a family-owned and operated business.

In less than two decades, Tapani Underground has grown from a $20,000-a-year business to a more than $20-million firm, with more than 90 employees.

The name Tapani Underground says it all—its work is mostly underground and unseen. But while what it does isn't always noticed, without its preparatory work, no building, parking lot, or road could be completed.

Tapani Underground has a fleet of more than 100 pieces of heavy equipment, from backhoes and excavators to loaders and scrapers. It specializes in road construction, both public and private; commercial and residential site development, including clearing lots, installing utilities, and grading the building pads and parking lots; and doing clearing, excavation, street work, and utilities for subdivisions.

In addition, Tapani Underground has built a solid reputation for its ability to install pump stations, sewer lines, and water lines. Beneath numerous commercial and industrial projects, are quality underground utilities and state-of-the-art road beds installed by Tapani Underground.

Located at 1904 Southeast Sixth Place in Battle Ground for more than a decade, Tapani Underground is more than just a trustworthy construction firm, it continues to be a family-owned and operated business. President and founder Iner Tapani has brought five of his sons into the business, and his wife, Beverly is the company secretary.

The company's success is built on experience: it knows the community and the variety of ground conditions it works in, critical when making a project bid. Safety is a priority at Tapani Underground, and a safety director visits every job several times over the course of a project to be certain workers adhere to safety guidelines.

And Tapani Underground, while it has seen phenomenal growth in the past two decades, still maintains a family-owned atmosphere for all its employees. Most of its work is done in Clark County, so employees don't have long commutes to job sites. Working locally means employees know that they aren't just on "any job," but are building the roads they will drive on, building schools their children will attend, or shopping malls they'll patronize. In this way, every employee of Tapani Underground takes just a little more pride in how the job gets done.

Tapani Underground's success depends on winning construction contracts in the community, so it understands the need to give something back. Nearly every job has some volunteer factor in it—some "little extra" not called for in the contract. And it donates regularly to local charities and organizations like the Washington State Patrol.

But the ultimate reason for the growth and success of Tapani Underground is that it approaches every job with the desire to treat the client fairly and honestly. Tapani Underground is the "Name You Can Trust" and every employee, from the president down is dedicated to keeping that trust in the community.

The name Tapani Underground says it all—its work is mostly underground and unseen. But while what it does isn't always noticed, without its preparatory work, no building, parking lot, or road could be completed.

North Coast Electric Company

North Coast Electric Company prides itself on achieving the growth and change necessary to meet its clients' requirements. It is this ability to move with the future that is the hallmark of North Coast Electric.

North Coast Electric Company has been aiding industrial customers, contractors, and homeowners for generations, providing them with industrial, residential, and commercial electrical materials. From bridgework to high-rise buildings, North Coast Electric has a definitive presence in the ever-changing landscape of Clark County.

Founded in 1913, North Coast Electric began with two small service centers in Portland and Seattle. Today, it has 28 service centers throughout the Pacific Northwest, in Washington, Oregon, Idaho, and Alaska, representing more than 200 manufacturers and with an inventory representing more than $20 million. North Coast employees number in excess of 500, and sales company-wide topped $200 million last year.

The service center in Vancouver, like all North Coast Electric Company centers, supplies contractors with everything for the electrical needs of a building, from transformers and switching gear to lighting and load centers, panel boards, fittings, circuit breakers, and pipes. Anything that has to do with an electrical connection can be found at North Coast.

North Coast is also moving quickly into the world of "data-com" and wiring for computer hookups. More and more new homes being built today want to be "wired for the 21st Century," and North Coast Electric has the capability to fulfill that need.

North Coast prides itself on being two steps ahead of its customers' needs, and having the latest in technology gives it a driving edge. Customers can order on-line, and with real-time computer inventory, they know literally up to the minute what is available in North Coast's warehouses. In fact, because bar coding on products makes purchase orders so expeditious and uncomplicated, several of the service centers are now considered "paperless."

In addition, North Coast Electric offers delivery of products right to the job site, and overnight delivery between service centers means that customers don't have to wait for shipment, even for infrequent or uncommon orders.

Remembering its social responsibilities, the Vancouver service center is a regular sponsor of charitable events. Whether it's sponsoring a Little League baseball team or providing anti-drug coloring books which the local police bureau hands out to children, North Coast Electric believes in giving back to the community that supports it.

Because it wants knowledgeable staff in all its service centers, North Coast Electric continually updates and expands training for its employees. Many take advantage of training schools by electrical product manufacturers, and North Coast also ensures its employees are proficient in both computer and Internet use. The company even pays 100 percent of the tuition costs for continuing adult education for its employees.

The only wholly family-owned electrical-products business of its kind, North Coast Electric generates loyalty among not only its customers, but also its employees, some of whom have worked there for 40 years.

North Coast Electric Company is a solid, integrity-based business whose dynamic approach secures its investment in the future. Quality service, up-to-date technology—North Coast truly lives up to its mission statement: To develop valuable and innovative partnerships that benefit customers, employees, and manufacturers. It is these attributes that establish North Coast Electric Company as the dominant electrical provider in the market today.

(above) North Coast Electric's service center in Vancouver, located on Northeast 60th Way, supplies contractors with everything for the electrical needs of a building, from transformers and switching gear to lighting and load centers, panel boards, fittings, circuit breakers, and pipe.

(below) With quality service and up-to-date technology, North Coast truly lives up to its mission statement: To develop valuable and innovative partnerships that benefit customers, employees, and manufacturers.

Otak and Killian Pacific

Downtown Vancouver is undergoing a revival in nearly every sense of the word, and two local architect/design and development firms are at the heart of the redevelopment bringing exciting changes to the city: Otak and Killian Pacific.

Killian Pacific is the developer behind a project designed to help create a downtown that is not only a place where people come to work, but also to live and play. The six-story, $21-million building on Sixth and Broadway, called the West Coast Bank Building, will house West Coast Bank as a major tenant and will also have public parking, additional office space, and upscale residential condominiums.

With a panoramic top floor view of Portland, Mt. Hood, and the river, it will be the kind of mixed-use building that will attract both businesses and residents, and create a welcoming entrance to the state of Washington and Vancouver's historic lower Main Street area.

For more than 30 years Killian Pacific has built a reputation as a premier commercial development firm receiving many accolades for its thoughtful, artistic, and high-quality developments. With projects all over the Portland and Vancouver area, including the Andresen Marketplace, Evergreen Marketplace and the Chart House, and Who-Song and Larry's restaurants, Killian Pacific has been a leader in Clark County's commercial real estate development.

A family-owned business with four full-time employees, it takes pride in picking projects that enhance the community. With the West Coast Bank Building project, Killian Pacific is taking the first step towards the redevelopment of downtown Vancouver that has potential for additional opportunities.

With a panoramic top-floor view of Portland, Mt. Hood, and the river, Killian Pacific's West Coast Bank Building will be the kind of mixed-use building that will attract both businesses and residents, and create a welcoming entrance to the state of Washington and Vancouver's historic lower Main Street area.

Vancouvercenter is a $60-million project designed by Otak that will include 192 apartments, 72 condominiums, 750 parking spaces, and 150,000 square feet of office and commercial space. With the Vancouvercenter Project, Otak has had a great influence on the rebirth of the city's downtown.

Another important new development going in downtown is Vancouvercenter, a $60-million project designed by Otak that will include 192 apartments, 72 condominiums, 750 parking spaces, and 150,000 square feet of office and commercial space.

Otak was founded in 1981 by three partners who sought to create a planning, engineering, and design firm that would set new standards. They've achieved that dream and more.

With the Vancouvercenter Project, Otak has had a great influence on the rebirth of the city's downtown. Located on part of the old Lucky Lager Brewery site, which the city bought, the project is being developed by Vandevco, a Washington corporation with ties to the United Arab Emirates.

Otak is designing the mixed-use project to include underground parking, apartments and condominiums, and office space. It's expected to be the "crown jewel" in the new downtown, but designed to complement current buildings. To encourage flow from downtown to the nearby Esther Short Park, Otak has included a park-like plaza through the heart of the project to encourage flow from downtown to the park. The undertaking will be built in three phases, but because Otak is the single designer, there will be consistency and unity throughout.

Otak is an award-winning consulting firm that has worked on such diverse projects as Light Rail, parks and greenways, multi-family and urban housing, and growth management.

Some of the more notable projects it has worked on include Forest Heights, Murray Hill mixed-use development, Westside Light Rail and the Central City Streetcar, Nike World Campus in Beaverton, Lloyd Place, and the Frank Estate.

With more than 200 professionals in offices located in Lake Oswego, Oregon, and Vancouver, Seattle, Kirkland, Washington, and Carbondale, Colorado, Otak offers its clients the full range of disciplines, from architecture, planning, engineering, surveying, and landscape architecture.

Otak and Killian Pacific. Two firms bringing their experience and talent to fulfill Vancouver's downtown redevelopment goals of creating a new and vital central area for the city.

Photo by Cliff Barbour

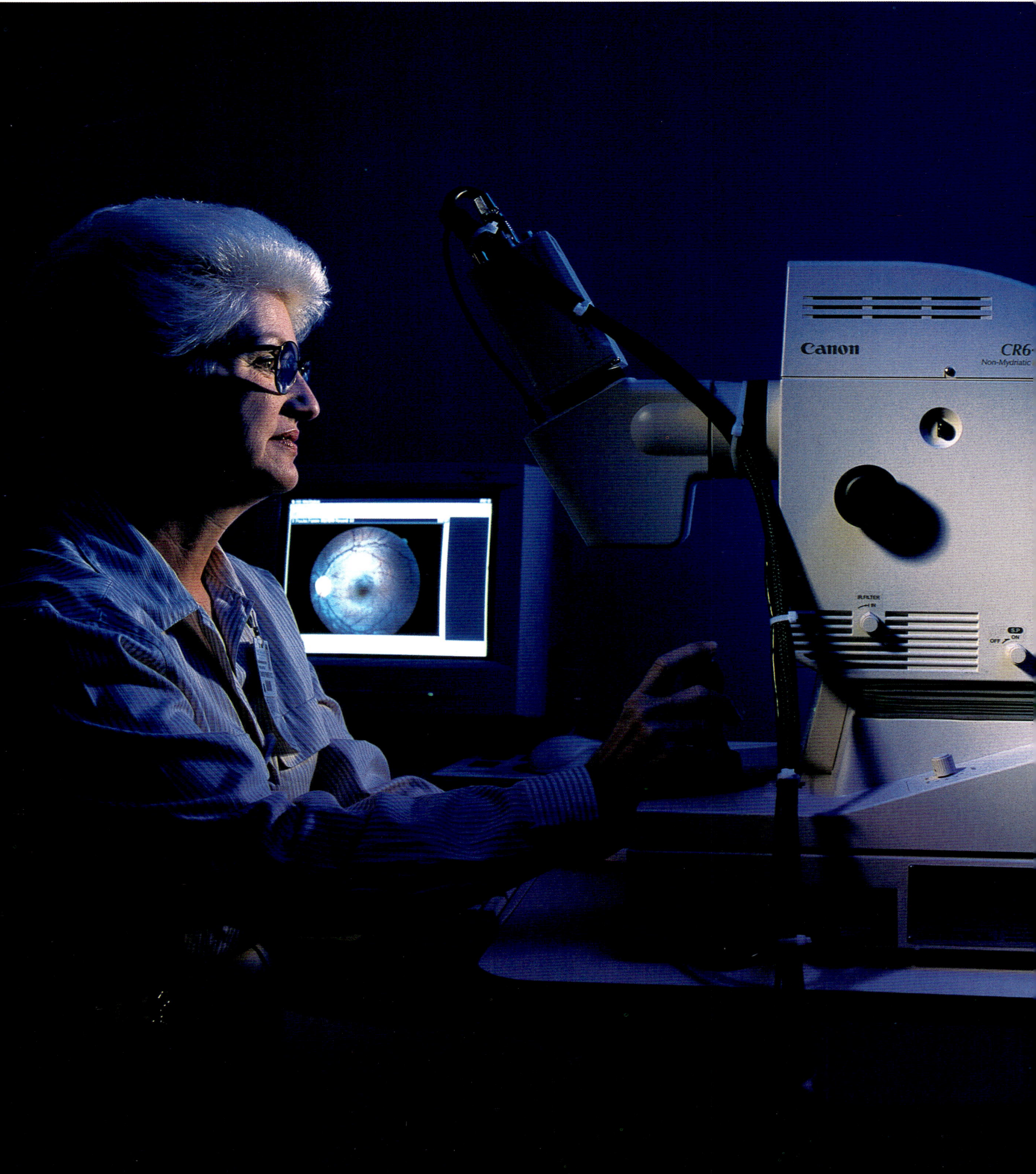

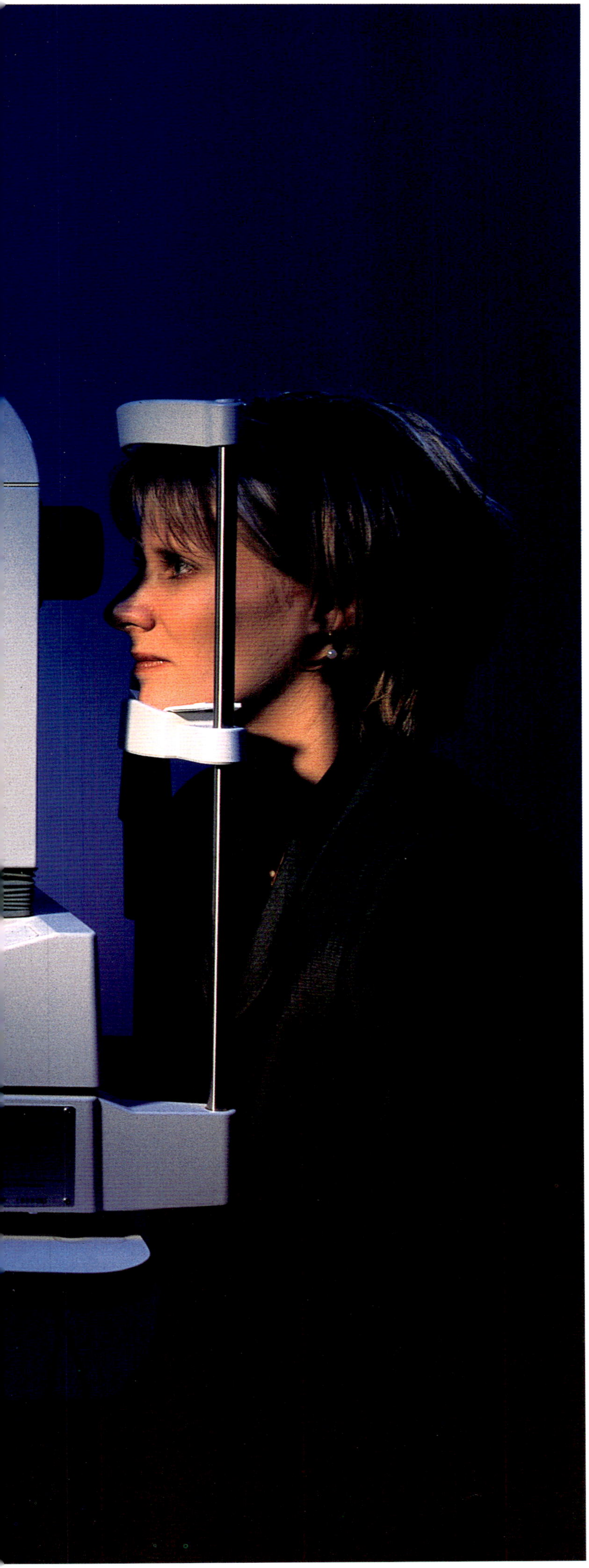

A Portrait of Prosperity

Health Care

Chapter 13

Southwest Washington Medical Center, 140

Wendel Family Dental Centre, 144

The Vancouver Clinic, 145

Kaiser Permanente, 146

(above) Photo courtesy of Kaiser Permanente

(left) Photo by Don Wheeler

Southwest Washington Medical Center

WHERE THE PATIENT COMES FIRST

When it comes to health care, the people who live and work in Clark County are fortunate to be served by Southwest Washington Medical Center (SWMC), a comprehensive medical center, that offers caring, compassionate staff and leading-edge technology—all right here in our own community.

(above) Growing with Clark County, SWMC more than doubled the original medical center site in 1991, including the new main entrance on Mother Joseph Place.

(right) SWMC's extensive rehabilitation program helps people of all ages. A young mother could play with her son again after rehab helped relieve severe dizziness caused by an accident.

SWMC is recognized as one of the Top 100 Hospitals in the nation by HCIA, a Baltimore-based health-care information agency. We think we know why. Because for our staff and volunteers, it is always the patient who comes first. We, who work and volunteer here, understand the human side of medicine is just as important as having the latest technology.

That's why you'll see the medical center's values of compassion, excellence, integrity, respect, and teamwork carefully reflected in each person's actions and care.

Southwest Washington Medical Center has a long, rich heritage in our region that dates back to the mid-1800s. For many of these years, two hospitals served the community. The first, St. Joseph Hospital, was established when Sister Joseph of the Sacred Heart opened the hospital in 1858. In 1967, the Sisters of Providence officially transferred the institution to the St. Joseph Community Hospital Association.

In 1929, Clark General Hospital began caring for patients in Vancouver. At the end of World War II, it was renamed Vancouver Memorial Hospital to honor veterans. After decades of working separately, the two hospitals merged in 1977, forming Southwest Washington Hospitals.

The name was changed in 1989 to Southwest Washington Medical Center, to better reflect our major expansion of services to our community.

Today, SWMC is a non-profit organization, governed by a community board of directors, individuals who work and live here and who understand best the need for a comprehensive medical center in Clark County. Because of our board's careful stewardship, residents do not have to leave the community to have all their health-care needs met.

EXPANDED SERVICES AT MORE LOCATIONS

Main Campus

Southwest Washington Medical Center's main campus is comprised of our full-service hospital and medical center with 360 licensed beds.

We provide all acute services for the county here. In fact, the SWMC Emergency Department is the busiest in the Portland metropolitan area and one of the busiest on the entire West Coast,

As one of the busiest birth centers in the region, SWMC welcomes nearly 5,000 babies a year in comfortable birthing rooms with highly trained staff.

with 77,000 emergency-room visits each year. That's due, in part, to Clark County's rapid growth, as well as our being the only provider of emergency care in the county.

SWMC also provides over 30 different types of medical services including neuro surgery, cardiac care including open-heart surgery, cancer care, trauma, rehabilitation, obstetrics, general medicine, and behavioral health care. On our main campus, the medical center's 11 surgical suites handle everything in the surgical arena except for organ transplants.

Our orthopedics program enjoys an outstanding national reputation. Excelling in all aspects of orthopedic medicine, the program qualifies as one of the top 100 orthopedic hospitals in the nation by HCIA. The orthopedic surgeons in the Vancouver-based Rebound group provide medical and surgical care for all the region's professional sports teams, including the Portland Trail Blazers and the Portland Winterhawks. Patients appreciate coming to one convenient center for all their orthopedic and rehabilitative care in a medical office building on the main hospital campus.

We welcome nearly 5,000 babies into the world each year at our Family Birth Center. As the second busiest birth center in the metropolitan region, we expanded our facility by 25,000 square feet in 1998 to grow our birth center to 49 beds including 32 integrated labor-delivery and postpartum rooms. Now mother, baby, and family can stay in one room through their entire childbirth experience. With a team of 90 physicians and midwives along with 180 staff members, the Family Birth Center is ready to serve our growing community for years and generations to come.

The Cancer Center of Southwest Washington provides comprehensive, convenient, and coordinated care right in our own community for those who face a cancer diagnosis. We offer a full array of treatments including surgery, medical-infusion oncology, radiation oncology, and the services of our excellent cancer immunology laboratory. Patients have access to the latest research and specialty treatments without leaving Clark County through our affiliation with Columbia River Oncology Project (CROP) and our partnership with Oregon Health Sciences University (OHSU).

The Cancer Center also has two state-of-the-art linear accelerators that allow doctors to focus high doses of radiation on the cancer, while protecting the surrounding tissues.

What makes a real difference for every patient is our dedicated professionals at the Cancer Center— doctors, nurses, support coordinators, and educators along with volunteers who truly make the difference by providing compassionate and individualized care for every patient.

SWMC's heart service was rated one of the top 100 heart programs in the county by HCIA. In addition to providing the latest in diagnostic procedures and rehabilitative care, SWMC's skilled cardiologists can perform vascular angiography and echocardiography at our medical center and a team of nationally-respected surgeons can perform open-heart surgery and life-saving cardiac procedures. Patients also have access to dietitians, physical therapists, social workers, and other specialists to monitor and guide their recovery following surgery.

Our Cardiac Rehabilitation Department, one of the first programs in the country to be accredited by the American Association of

Complete diagnostic services include an open and conventional MRI, helical CT scanners, PET and nuclear medicine scanners, certified mammography and stereotactic breast imaging, bone densitometry, ultrasound, x-ray, and cardiovascular angiography suites.

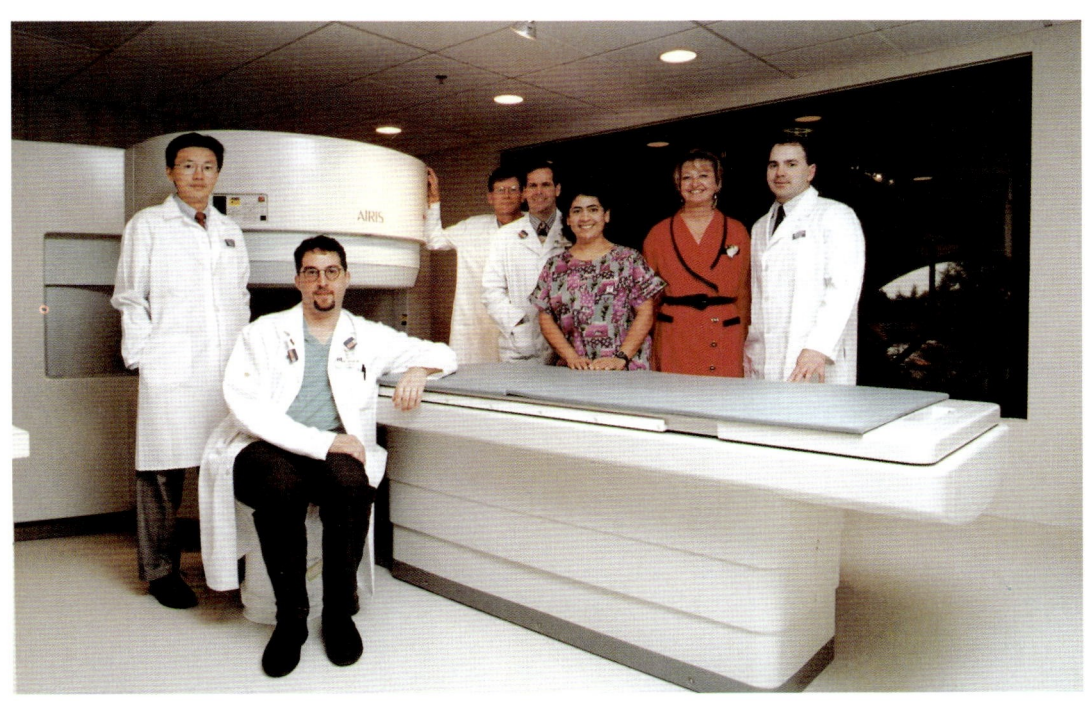

Cardiovascular and Pulmonary Rehabilitation, helps patients reduce symptoms and avoid future heart attacks.

Our medical center also offers a family-medicine training program for 18 residents who receive their experience through the Family Medicine of Southwest Washington clinic. The residents and nine faculty members operate this clinic to provide medical care to residents in Southwest Washington.

Faculty members, all of whom have clinical faculty appointments at the University of Washington, help make the Family Medicine Residency one of the rotation's top-rated training programs.

We also believe in providing information to promote wellness and healthy living. Our main campus is home to superb education services so our community can get reliable, complete health-care information. Our library is linked to a wide network of health and community libraries, an interactive Web site, and our medical professionals offer a comprehensive array of community-education classes, all in our community-education center.

We are pleased to have earned a reputation for excellence in diagnostic imaging. In addition to both conventional and open MRIs, we offer leading-edge mammography, bone densitometry, nuclear medicine, ultrasound, CT, and PET services to the community.

Memorial Health Center

Our Memorial Health Center is a specialized community health center on Vancouver's west side in the former Memorial Hospital. A major renovation in 1998 changed the variety of services offered at this campus. It now houses medical offices; psychiatric services; inpatient, outpatient, and partial-hospitalization mental-health programs; outpatient surgery; and physical therapy and pain management services.

Our newly remodeled and expanded urgent-care facility offers 11 total treatment rooms and a well-planned, enjoyable space to allow staff to treat minor injuries and illnesses around the clock every day.

The Urgent Care Clinic at Memorial provides 24-hour, 7-day service for minor illness and injury.

Memorial Health Center also has one of the most comprehensive hospice centers, providing in-home care and comfort for those with terminal illnesses and their families.

The Health Connection, a community health library, on the Memorial Campus gives residents on-line research assistance and community-education resources in their own neighborhood.

Healthy Steps

We are committed to supporting the neediest in our community with excellent and compassionate care. Healthy Steps Women's and Children's Center reflects our hospital's mission to provide affordable care for the most vulnerable in the community. Nurse practitioners and midwives provide medical care and prenatal and obstetrical care for more than 20,000 women and children each year. Healthy Steps has multi-lingual staff to serve the region's growing minority populations.

Rehabilitation's Rooftop Garden

An inviting, soothing environment can make such a difference in a patient's recovery. Thanks to the Crossroads Community Church and SWMC's Physical Medicine and Rehabilitation program, patients recovering from strokes, accidents, or other illnesses find solace and serenity in our Rooftop Garden. Local artists and community leaders transformed an ordinary rooftop into a serene, natural environment right next to our inpatient rehabilitation unit. The Rooftop Garden helps take the "clinical" atmosphere out of recovery and puts in its place a little refuge of nature.

Rehab patients recovering from stroke, accident, or other illness find a touch of nature in the Rooftop Garden created by local artists and community leaders.

PARTNERING FOR OUR COMMUNITY

SWMC and Kaiser Permanente have a long-standing partnership to share expertise, resources, and experience for the betterment of Clark County residents. Kaiser insures about 30 percent of the county's population, but has no hospital here, so it contracts with SWMC for most inpatient services.

A major joint venture will change the feel and look of health care in Southwest Washington when three top health-care providers come together. SWMC, Northwest Surgical Specialists, and The Vancouver Clinic are creating a new ambulatory surgical center, scheduled to open in late 2000.

This new outpatient facility will include 10 surgical suites, making it one of the largest surgi-centers on the West Coast, capable of offering important surgeries, from knee reconstruction and spine surgeries, to sinus procedures and plastic surgery. The unique collaboration of these three health-care providers will mean patients will have convenient, compassionate care and state-of-the-art technology in a cost-effective setting.

(above) Healthy Steps Women's and Children's Center serves those who might not otherwise be able to afford health care. A multilingual staff eases concerns for Clark County's growing minority population.

(below) World-renowned heart surgeon, Albert Krause, M.D. (second from left), heads a stellar team of heart surgeons, nurses, and technicians.

WE'RE COMMITTED TO OUR COMMUNITY

How do you build a healthier community? Not only by offering excellent medical care, but also by supporting organizations that make a difference in the health of Clark County residents.

The Southwest Washington Medical Center Foundation makes financial contributions to such organizations as Community Choices 2010 and the Free Clinic—programs that help educate us about how to make healthy choices in our lifestyles, improve our well-being, and provide medical support for our community's families in need. We know it is not enough to deal with the "end result" of poor health, and that our entire community benefits when preventive health is a priority.

As the major health-care provider for our community, and our community's only hospital, we take our role very seriously. We believe we have an even greater responsibility to provide the best care available to our neighbors and coworkers in Clark County.

We live here, work here, and care about the health of our community's future. We're committed to providing the right care, right in our community.

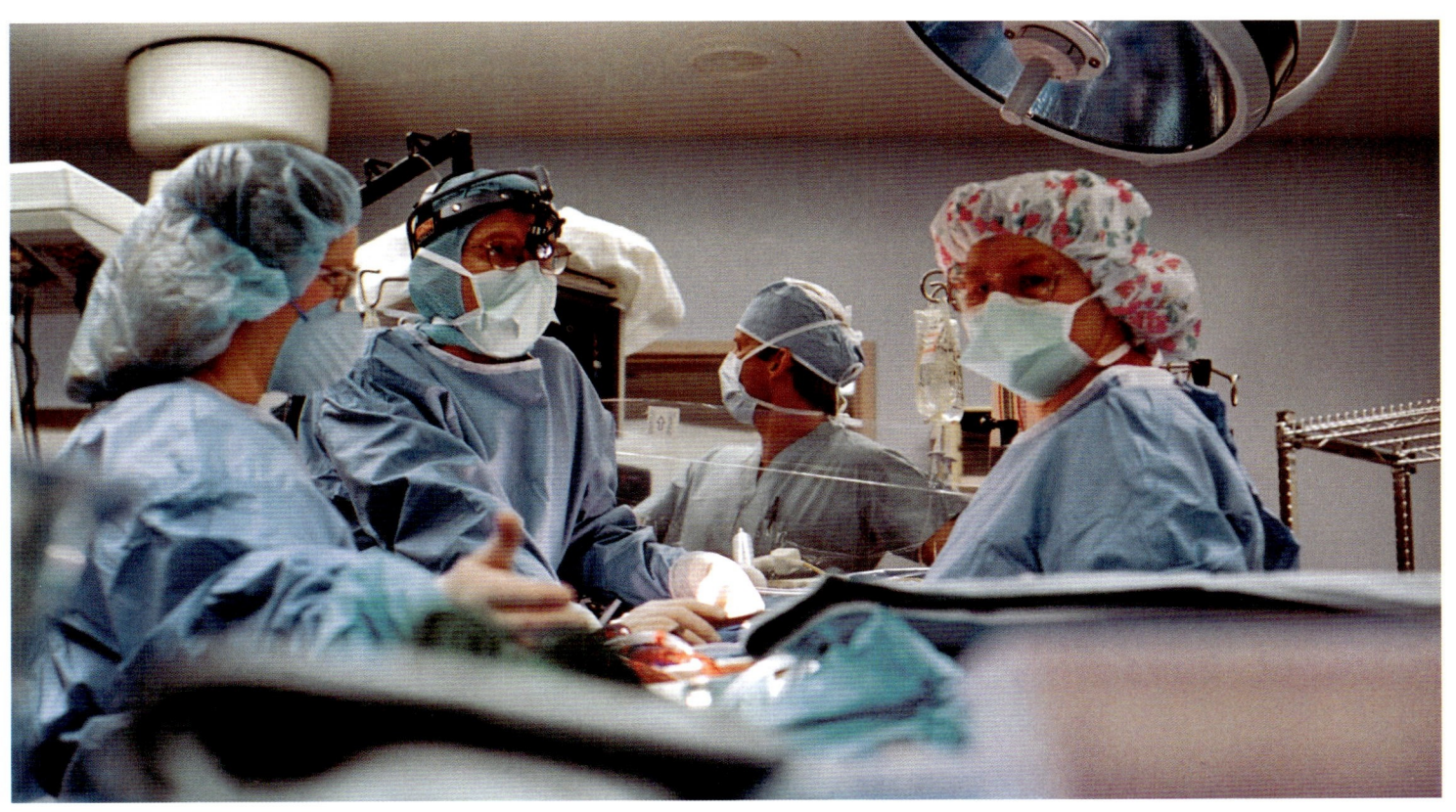

Wendel Family Dental Centre

Wendel Family Dental Centre offers excellent, caring dental service—general dentistry, cosmetic dentistry, orthodontics, dentures, and much more. With its multiple offices, plus early morning, evening, and Saturday appointments available, clients are sure to find it easy and convenient to have all their dental work taken care of.

There are three Wendel Family Dental Centres: Fisher's Landing at 1499 Southeast Tech Center Place, which has eight operatories and three dentists; Salmon Creek at 1300 Northeast 134th Street, with seven operatories and two dentists; and the largest, Vancouver, located at 7012 Northeast 40th Street, with 24 operatories and 13 dentists.

But bigger doesn't mean fast, impersonal service. Clients don't feel like just a number in a "dental mill" when they visit a Wendel Family Dental Centre. The centre's philosophy is to always make each client feel like an individual and to offer its services in a manner which reflects the utmost respect and consideration for each person.

One way it can keep that commitment is to use a "team" approach at Wendel Family Dental Centres. Each office has teams made up of three dentists who work closely together on cases. This gives patients another experienced choice for treatment should their regular dentist be unavailable, without fearing that they'll get someone who doesn't know them.

Since Wendel Family Dental Centres are not a part of any dental insurance program, but operate on a fee-for-service basis, clients and selected PPOs come to them because they choose to, not because they must. That's why excellent customer care and service is paramount to the entire operation, and a key component of their vision statement.

When clients visit a Wendel Family Dental Centre, they know they will receive the very latest in dental technology. Whether it's any dental treatments, or the tiny intraoral cameras, which allow dentists and clients a better view of teeth, or IV sedation for greater pain control, the dentists are committed to keeping up with the latest techniques to provide superior service.

In fact, Wendel Family Dental Centre sends its dentists to continuing education throughout the year, and even teaches an American General Dentists Association certified course on IV sedation every other year. But every technique used is proven, not experimental, to ensure quality and safety for clients.

Wendel Family Dental Centre is committed to taking an active part in the community as well, with participation in such groups as Rotary, Chamber of Commerce, and YWCA, or by hosting blood drives twice a year for the American Red Cross.

Is it any wonder that some of its dentists have been working at Wendel Family Dental Centres for more than 10 years? Or that staff turnover is remarkably low? Or that so many clients have made Wendel Family Dental Centres their home for all their dental needs for so many years?

Word of mouth and superior dental service have made Wendel Family Dental Centre the only choice for thousands of southwest Washington families.

Part of the Family.

The Vancouver Clinic

The Vancouver Clinic has a long-standing history as Clark County's largest private, multi-specialty healthcare clinic. For more than 64 years, The Vancouver Clinic has served the families of Vancouver and its surrounding communities, by providing comprehensive medical services and keeping the uncompromising and compassionate care of its patients as its first priority and ongoing mission.

In 1936, comprehensive family healthcare was the vision of the Obstetrician/Gynecologist, Pediatrician, Internist, and Surgeon who founded The Vancouver Clinic. The multi-specialty model selected was first used by the world-famous Mayo Clinic. Today, that vision remains predominate as evidenced by over 125,000 individuals and their families who seek healthcare from The Vancouver Clinic's broad range of medical services.

As the Vancouver/Clark County area has rapidly expanded in size and population, The Vancouver Clinic proactively grows to keep pace with its demand for services. Five separate Vancouver Clinics now serve their patients in the communities of Battle Ground (Highway 502), Fisher's Landing (McGillivray Boulevard), and Salmon Creek (NE 129th, off Highway 99), in addition to its main facility located in the Garrison Heights neighborhood, one block west of Southwest Washington Medical Center.

Recruitment for the best physician candidates and expanding access to medical service in Clark County are ongoing priorities at The Vancouver Clinic. The medical staff includes many doctors from renowned training universities such as Stanford, University of Washington, Oregon Health Sciences University, and the Mayo Clinic. Forty-seven primary-care doctors and 14 associate providers (physician assistants, certified nurse midwives, and nurse practitioners) offer healthcare in the areas of Obstetrics/Gynecology, Pediatrics, Family Practice, and Internal Medicine. They are complimented by 38 specialty physicians who offer patients expertise in the areas of Cardiology, Dermatology, Ear, Nose, and Throat, Endocrinology, Facial Plastic Surgery, Gastroenterology, Infectious Disease, Nephrology, Occupational Medicine, Pulmonology, Rheumatology, Surgery, and Urgent Care. One hundred percent of The Vancouver Clinic's doctors are Board Certified or Board eligible.

The Vancouver Clinic provides continuity of care to its patients by providing ancillary services on-site. This consolidated delivery system is much more convenient and cost effective for its patients. Ancillary services and mini-clinics include: Bone Densitometry, Coumadin Clinic, Foot Care Clinic, Health Resource Library, Infusion Center, Laboratory, Diagnostic Imaging—Mammography, Ultrasound, and X-ray, and Physical Therapy.

Some of The Vancouver Clinic's other notable services include:
- Occupational Medicine, which offers pre-employment physicals, drug testing, Federal Aviation Medical Exams, as well as on-the-job injury and physical therapy for workers.
- A Travel Clinic offers pre- and post-travel health counseling, medications, immunizations, and medical documents for overseas travel.
- Magnetic Resonance Imaging (MRI) provides on-site scans with the most state-of-the-art equipment available on the market.
- The Endoscopy Center is a state-licensed, Medicare-approved outpatient clinic for patients needing a colonoscopy or upper endoscopic exam.
- Two of clinic's surgeons have received training in Laproscopic Bariatric Bypass Surgery, (a surgical procedure for obesity). Currently, they are the only Clark County practitioners performing this type of surgery.
- The Clinical Trials Research Department cooperates with pharmaceutical companies providing patients and physicians the opportunity to participate in FDA approved medical drug trials and exposure to the newest advances in pharmaceutical medicine.

The Vancouver Clinic is proud of the patient care its physicians and staff of 430 provide—it's what draws people back. The clinic's business is people, and taking care of them, but its commitment to the community regularly extends beyond the walls of its own medical clinics. Staff and providers regularly sponsor and participate in community events, like Race for The Cure®, United Way, Vancouver Walk for Diabetes, and the American Heart Walk.

The Vancouver Clinic strives to be the best place in Clark County to receive medical care. New technology, continuous education, improved customer services, top-rated recruitment, and advanced treatment opportunities, assure the delivery of high-quality care to its patients in a constantly changing healthcare industry.

Kaiser Permanente

Kaiser Permanente is the largest and most experienced health-care delivery system of its kind in the nation. As a not-for-profit, prepaid, group-practice health-care organization, Kaiser Permanente stresses preventive care to keep its members healthy.

An extensive award-winning clinical information system at Kaiser Permanente provides physicians and other staff with instant access to comprehensive patient information.

The program has deep roots in Washington State. In 1938, industrialist Henry Kaiser and his son Edgar invited Sidney Garfield, MD, to bring a group of physicians to Eastern Washington to care for workers building the Grand Coulee Dam.

In the hectic days following the attack on Pearl Harbor, as America geared up for war, tens of thousands of workers poured into Clark County seeking jobs in the Kaiser shipyards.

Kaiser promised his workers jobs, decent housing, and comprehensive medical care. He again turned to Dr. Garfield to help provide health care. They used the same system that had worked so well before: Workers paid a small amount each month to receive complete health care for themselves and their families.

It was comprehensive care from the first-aid stations at the shipyards to a brand-new hospital built amid prune orchards in east Vancouver. At the height of the war, the Northern Permanente Foundation Hospital served 30,000 workers and their family members for 50 cents a month paid by workers.

The war ended in 1945; however, the demand for quality health care at an affordable price did not. Henry Kaiser and Dr. Garfield agreed to continue their novel health plan and opened membership to the general community. Growth came as quickly as the new Baby-Boom Generation throughout the 1950s, and today Kaiser Permanente has more than 90,000 Clark County members enrolled in its medical plan and another 35,000 in its dental plan.

Kaiser Permanente offers treatment at four Clark County medical offices:

Cascade Park Medical Office, 12607 Southeast Mill Plain Boulevard.
Fisher's Landing Medical Office, 16703 Southeast McGillivray Boulevard.
Salmon Creek Medical Office, 14406 Northeast 20th Avenue.
Vancouver Medical Office, 2211 East Mill Plain Boulevard.

Each medical office provides primary care services (family practice, internal medicine, and pediatrics), health education, pharmacy, laboratory, radiology, and social services. A range of specialty services is offered at one or more offices, including dermatology, general surgery, Ob/Gyn, occupational health, ophthalmology, and urgent care.

Two dental offices also serve Kaiser Permanente members living in Clark County:

The **Cascade Park Dental Office**, at 12711 Southeast Mill Plain Boulevard, provides general dentistry services as well as orthodontics and pedodontics.

The **Salmon Creek Dental Office**, at 14406 Northeast 20th Avenue, offers general dentistry services along with endodontics, periodontics, and denturist services.

Kaiser Permanente's membership growth in Clark County is the fastest of any county in the Northwest. The program is the choice among the area's most prominent employers, including SEH America, Sharp Electronics Corp., the Clark Public Utilities, *The Columbian*, the Evergreen School District, and the City of Vancouver.

Kaiser Permanente staff are committed to the community, living in Clark County as well as working there—over one thousand of them, including physicians, dentists, nurses, and technicians.

Kaiser Permanente is also committed to the well-being of the community it serves. Employees are active in such organizations as Community Choices 2010, the Free Clinic, the Chamber of Commerce, and the Clark County YWCA, to name just a few. In this way, Kaiser Permanente continues giving to a community it has been a part of for more than 55 years.

Kaiser Permanente's Health Resource Center offers its members health-related books, videos, health-education handouts, access to health-related Internet sites, and referrals to Kaiser Permanente classes and community resources.

Photo by Cliff Barbour

A Portrait of Prosperity

Education

Chapter 14

"A book is a wonderful invention, as basic as the wheel. One doesn't have to plug a book in, one doesn't have to thaw it out; one simply opens it, and another human being speaks to you."

—Lewis D. Cannell

Clark College, 150

Clark County's Educational Community, 152

(left) The Lewis D. Cannell Library is a Clark College campus landmark. Photos by Kevin Williams

149

Clark College

Built upon more than a half-century of traditions and values linked to Vancouver's past, Clark College is the place current residents look to find the future.

Whether they need short-term skills training, technical certification, or transfer credits toward a bachelor's degree, students at Clark College receive quality instruction combining state-of-the-art technology with current research.

Professor Keith Stansbury directs students working on an electronics and robotics project in one of Clark's state-of-the-art technology labs.

Fourth largest in the Washington State system of 35 community and technical colleges, Clark serves more than 12,500 full-time and part-time students each quarter. It is an attractive choice for those seeking an affordable alternative to private colleges or university undergraduate programs, to complete lower division coursework while living at home.

A wide range of class times makes Clark College the place to advance a career while still employed. Taking only evening courses, a student can earn an associate degree or complete one of several technical-training programs. Vancouver residents of all ages, including senior citizens, also take advantage of day and evening classes for personal enjoyment and self-improvement.

READY FOR THE JOB MARKET IN ONE OR TWO YEARS

From humble beginnings in 1933 when it offered just a half-dozen academic courses in a turn-of-the century converted house, Clark College has earned a reputation for excellence in vocational and academic studies at its scenic 80-acre campus in Vancouver's historic Central Park.

Students may complete one- or two-year certificate programs that prepare them for technical careers in a variety of fields, from microcomputer specialist to Web author, from commercial chef to administrative assistant.

Clark College offers two-year associate degrees in 40 different technical/professional majors, including accounting, business administration and technology, automotive and diesel repair, early childhood education, machining, paralegal, and restaurant management. Local high-tech industries provide instructional resources and equipment for those training in data networks and telecommunications, electronics, computer networking, and software development. Those seeking careers in health care can select accredited programs in nursing and dental hygiene, pharmacy assisting, and phlebotomy.

For students planning to earn a four-year degree, lower division coursework and general education requirements for almost any major can be completed at Clark College. Graduates are well prepared for upper division classes. Reports show that Clark transfer students earn GPAs comparable to students who entered a four-year university directly from high school. Transfer agreements with all Washington public universities and several Oregon colleges ensure students receive full credit value for their Clark College studies.

Since 1989, Clark College has worked closely with the Washington State University Vancouver branch campus. Students are guided by advisors at both colleges in planning their course of studies and in securing financial aid. This partnership helps students transfer easily and enables them to stay in their home community. It also prevents a "brain drain," which means local businesses will have a talented and diverse pool of applicants for jobs. They can connect through Clark College's Student Employment Center, serving all students, graduates, and the public, which matches job seekers with prospective employers.

All Clark College students have access to two dozen modern computer labs, like this one in Scarpelli Hall.

QUALIFIED STAFF

More than 80 percent of the 148 full-time faculty at Clark College hold graduate degrees. Many conduct research in their fields of expertise, and vocational instructors hold industry certifications as well. All are devoted to helping students succeed. Approximately 300 adjunct faculty teach part-time at Clark, including community professionals with special expertise.

Faculty members preside over their own lab and conference sessions as well as lectures. Smaller classes mean students and instructors get to know each other, which creates a stronger learning environment and exchange of ideas.

Faculty also serve as academic advisors for students majoring in their field and often act as sponsors for college clubs and activities. Instructors stay in touch with changes in technology and the job market by serving on boards of professional organizations related to their educational fields.

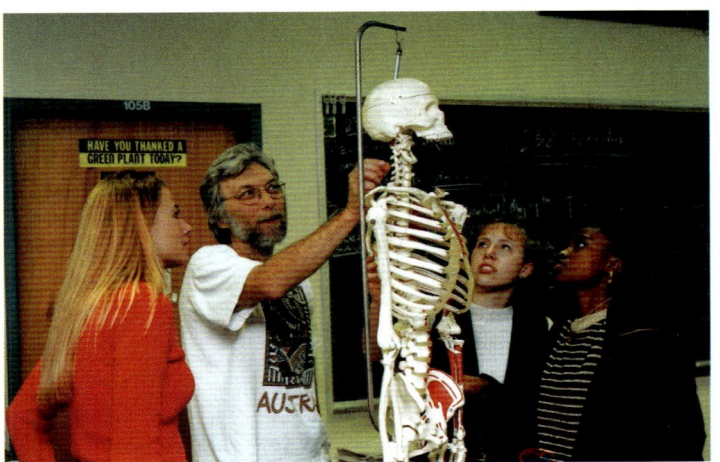

A strong core of science courses prepares students for Clark's regionally recognized health-care programs.

PARTNERSHIPS THAT WORK

Partnerships are a key to the success of many Clark College programs. Through agreements with business, public service agencies, and other education providers, Clark can better meet the needs of its students and prospective employers by ensuring that graduates have acquired the knowledge needed in today's workplace.

Each Clark College vocational program is supported by an advisory committee comprised of professionals working in the related industry. They serve as advisors to faculty on program curriculum and as mentors and contacts for students seeking internship opportunities and employment after graduation.

Clark College participates in several state-sponsored programs—Workforce Training, Workfirst, and Displaced Homemakers—designed to help adults who are making transitions in today's changing job market. Along with careful counseling, participants brush up skills in English, math, and beginning computer operation to qualify

Musicians from several generations share a love of music in Clark's instrumental and vocal performance groups and classes.

for entry-level employment or college training programs.

The College also helps local businesses and industries provide advanced training for their current employees by sending faculty to teach on site or developing classes on campus to meet a specific employer need. Another way the College assists employers is through English-As-A-Second Language courses and specialized training for professionals immigrating from other countries who need credentials to work in their new homeland

Collaboration with local high schools means Clark College can avoid duplication of services, saving tax dollars and reducing "redundant" coursework for students.

Clark College is particularly proud of its successful Running Start program, which allows high school juniors and seniors to take college-level courses that count toward high school diploma requirements and a college degree. About 600 students, representing all 23 high schools in the Clark College service area, participate each quarter.

Other high school students get a head start by taking part in the Advanced Placement Articulation/Tech Prep program. Those students who earn good grades in high school vocational classes can receive college credit and even advanced placement in related programs at the College.

Clark College views its role as a member of the Vancouver community seriously. It is proud to provide more than 1,500 local jobs, making it the 10th largest employer in Clark County. In addition to serving the educational needs of area residents, the campus gives the community access to cultural and civic events year round. Art exhibits, musical concerts, theatrical performances, educational lectures, and community-issues forums sponsored by Clark College are open to local residents as well.

HELPING BUILD FUTURES

In today's workplace, post-high school education is a necessity. Clark College enjoys a strong reputation in the Vancouver business community for its commitment to training students to become productive members of the local workforce. With a 60-year record of helping southwest Washington residents build profitable futures, there is no doubt Clark College will continue to provide the foundation for growth well into the 21st century.

Vancouver

Clark County's Educational Community

Parents, students, educators, and business all agree: The state of education in Clark County is very healthy, indeed. With nine public school districts and two state-run schools for special-needs children, the county is meeting challenges head on and looking toward a bright future.

BATTLE GROUND SCHOOL DISTRICT 119

Battle Ground enjoys several partnerships with its district, including an award-winning training program for fire cadets. The Center for Agriculture, Science, and Environmental Education (CASEE) partners with the Washington Department of Natural Resources, Washington State University Extension, and others to offer students everything from agrarian education to stream restoration. And the passage of a 1998 levy ensures local resources for programs and operations.

CAMAS SCHOOL DISTRICT 117

Passage of special technology levies has allowed Camas School District to upgrade its infrastructure, have access to a kaleidoscope of high-tech possibilities, and offer an exemplary student-to-computer ratio of six to one.

Camas's success is also exemplified by its test scores that consistently exceed state averages, its dynamic curriculum that makes learning relevant for all students, its continual improvement across grade levels, its solid education of basic skills, and its strong partnerships with local businesses.

EDUCATIONAL SERVICE DISTRICT 112

Educational Service District 112 is an integral partner to public education in Washington. It saves taxpayers millions each year through cooperative buying programs and regional services, offering more than 200 programs from staff development to insurance pooling. ESD 112 also administers local district cooperatives for at-risk youth and operates 23 child care centers in three counties.

EVERGREEN SCHOOL DISTRICT 114

The Evergreen School District is nationally recognized for its leadership in the field of education. It believes in high standards, academic achievement, and public accountability. Evergreen helps ensure success for all students through partnerships with families and the community.

In addition to a solid basic education program, Evergreen boasts a wide-ranging character education curriculum and a variety of extra-curricular programs. These programs are continuously evaluated and improved through Evergreen's staff development program, which is among the best in the nation.

GREEN MOUNTAIN SCHOOL DISTRICT 103

The smallest of the county's districts, Green Mountain School District serves 126 children in kindergarten through eighth grade. While its 75-year-old school facility maintains the country flavor of a rural community, the district leaves little wanting when it comes to high tech. It offers computers in every classroom as well as a low student-to-teacher ratio. Understanding the value of a strong early education program, Green Mountain puts special focus on reading.

HOCKINSON SCHOOL DISTRICT 98

Hockinson boasts an outstanding partnership with parents, with more volunteers in the classrooms than most school districts. This is one reason why Hockinson also has the highest test scores in the county and among the top in the entire state. Yet Hockinson is the largest district in the state without a high school to call its own. This will change however thanks to the approval of a bond issue in March of 2000. The district will build a new high school for its nearly 2,000 students.

LA CENTER SCHOOL DISTRICT 101

This 1,400-student district knows that the arts are a vital part of a well-rounded curriculum. La Center High partners with artists in the community for the La Center Arts Crawls. The high school's drama department, band, and jazz ensembles have received numerous awards. Academics are a priority as well. La Center Middle School is a training site for "Operation Physics" curriculum, and K-8 students participate in a science consortium as part of a $1.2-million National Science Foundation Grant.

RIDGEFIELD SCHOOL DISTRICT 122

An increasingly diverse and growing student population has prompted the Ridgefield School District to expand proven programs and add new ones to give students the most learning opportunities possible. These opportunities include: Project WRITE, a district-wide writing program; vocational programs at the high school and the Clark County Vocational Skills Center; and Partnerships in Elementary Science (PESE), a cooperative effort with other districts, Hewlett-Packard, and others, providing instruction to elementary students in physical, earth, and life sciences.

VANCOUVER PUBLIC SCHOOLS 37

As editorialized in *The Columbian* newspaper, strong community support for the Vancouver School District reflects a "proven track record in offering high-quality and innovative educational programs, in turning out well-prepared students, and in involving parents at almost every level of decision-making."

More than 1,000 partners and $13 million in private donations over the past several years help support Vancouver schools. Voters routinely approve levy and bond measures to provide a stable financial base. Student achievement scores exceed state and national averages, more than 1,350 students are enrolled in the district's popular magnet programs, and 83 percent of students plan to continue their education beyond high school.

WASHINGTON STATE SCHOOL FOR THE DEAF

Washington State School for the Deaf is both a public school and a state agency. The Campus School offers quality education to approximately 150 deaf and hard-of-hearing students ages 3 through 21 many of whom participate in the five day per week residential program.

As an agency, WSD offers support to the 2,000 to 3,000 deaf and hard-of-hearing students attending public schools throughout the state of Washington. WSD emphasizes integration of its students into the local community, fostering pride in students and their families, and serving as a statewide resource to children, families, and professionals.

WASHINGTON STATE SCHOOL FOR THE BLIND

Washington State School for the Blind specializes in providing quality educational services to blind and visually impaired children from throughout the state of Washington. The school serves as a statewide demonstration and resource center providing direct and indirect services to students both on the campus and in the children's local communities. Services are provided to families, educators, and others interested in assisting visually impaired youth in becoming independent contributing citizens. The school also serves as a statewide technology center, and statewide Braille Access Center that has produced over four million pages of Braille since 1990. Visit the school's Web site at www.wssb.wa.gov.

WASHOUGAL SCHOOL DISTRICT 112-6

Washougal School District offers comprehensive K-12 education through a variety of academic and alternative programs, including an alternative high school and learning center offering high school curricula, sixth through eighth grade accelerated math, home school support, fee-based credit recovery, and technology courses.

Washougal's Community Education program offers more than 50 classes quarterly for area residents, including computers, dance, first aid/CPR, money management, and foreign languages.

Thanks to the district's voters, a $36-million bond was passed in 1999. Washougal School District is in the process of upgrading and modernizing its facilities, including construction of a new middle school, to meet the needs of the 21st century.

Enterprise Index

Boise Cascade
907 W 7th Street
Vancouver, Washington 98660
Phone: 360-690-7000
Fax: 360-690-7052
www.bc.com
Pages 112-113

Bonneville Power Administration
PO Box 491
Vancouver, Washington 98666-0491
Phone: 360-418-8008
Fax: 360-418-8433
www.transmission.bpa.gov
Pages 96-97

Century 21 Complete Realty
416 NE 112th Avenue
Vancouver, Washington 98684
Phone: 360-254-1917
Fax: 360-254-2704
E-mail: realestate@c21complete.com
www.c21complete.com
Page 133

Clark College
1800 E McLoughlin Boulevard
Vancouver, Washington 98663
Phone: 360-992-2000
Fax: 360-992-2891
E-mail: webmaster@clark.edu
www.clark.edu
Pages 150-151

Clark County School Employees Credit Union
PO Box 1739
Vancouver, Washington 98668
Phone: 360-695-3441
Toll-free: 800-247-4364
Fax: 360-695-3658
E-mail: info@ccsecu.com
www.ccsecu.com
Page 129

Clark County's Educational Community
Educational Service District 112
2500 NE 65th Avenue
Vancouver, Washington 98661-6812
Phone: 360-750-7500
Fax: 360-750-9706
E-mail: lori.simpson@esd112.k12.wa.us
www.esd112.wednet.edu
Pages 152-153

Columbia Credit Union
PO Box 324
Vancouver, Washington 98666-0324
Phone: 360-891-4000
www.columbiacu.org
Pages 122-123

ConAgra Malt: Great Western Malting Company
1701 Industrial Way
Vancouver, Washington 98660
Phone: 360-693-3661
Fax: 360-699-9381
Page 116

Design Showroom, Inc.
1115 Esther Street, Suite D
Vancouver, Washington 98660
Phone: 360-693-5636
Fax: 360-693-5916
E-mail: design@pcez.com
Page 127

Greater Vancouver Chamber of Commerce
404 E 15th Street, Suite 11
Vancouver, Washington 98663
Phone: 360-694-2588
Fax: 360-693-8279
E-mail: chamber@vancouverusa.com
www.vancouverusa.com
Pages 120-121

Kaiser Permanente
500 NE Multnomah Street, Suite 100
Portland, Oregon 97232-2099
Phone: 503-813-4820
Fax: 503-813-4576
www.kp.org/nw
Page 146

Killian Pacific
811 NW 19th Avenue, Suite 102
Portland, Oregon 97209
Phone: 503-227-0423
Fax: 503-227-0471
E-mail: killianpacific@uswest.net
Page 136

Kyocera Industrial Ceramics Corporation
5713 E 4th Plain Boulevard
Vancouver, Washington 98661
Phone: 360-696-8950
Fax: 360-696-9804
E-mail: bob.osmun@kyocera.com
www.kyocera.com
Page 115

Lacamas Community Credit Union
236 NE 4th Avenue
PO Box 1108
Camas, Washington 98607
Phone: 360-834-3611
Fax: 360-834-7951
E-mail: service@lacamas.org
www.lacamas.org
Page 128

LSW Architects, P.C.
2300 Main Street
Vancouver, Washington 98660
Phone: 360-694-8571
Fax: 360-694-9510
E-mail: jwyckoff@lsw-architects.com
www.lsw-architects.com
Pages 124-125

New Edge Networks
3000 Columbia House Boulevard, Suite 106
Vancouver, Washington 98661
Phone: 877-725-3343
Fax: 360-693-9997
www.newedgenetworks.com
Pages 102-103

Norris, Beggs & Simpson
805 Broadway, Suite 700
Vancouver, Washington 98660
Phone: 360-699-7181
Fax: 360-690-4531
www.nbsrealtors.com
Page 132

North Coast Electric Company
12000 NE 60th Way
Vancouver, Washington 98682-5895
Phone: 360-253-2215
Fax: 360-253-2045
E-mail: sales21@ncelec.com
www.ncelec.com
Page 135

Otak
105 W Evergreen Boulevard, Suite 300
Vancouver, Washington 98660
Phone: 360-737-9613
Fax: 360-737-9651
www.otak.com
Page 136

Ray Hickey: Hickey Family Company
1499 SE Tech Center Place, Suite 140
Vancouver, Washington 98683
Phone: 360-604-4333
Fax: 360-604-4343
Pages 100-101

Sharp
5700 NW Pacific Rim Boulevard
Camas, Washington 98607
Phone: 360-834-8700
Fax: 360-834-8903
www.sharpsma.com
Pages 108-109

Southwest Washington Medical Center
400 NE Mother Joseph Place
PO Box 1600
Vancouver, Washington 98682
Phone: 360-514-3105
Fax: 360-514-2230
E-mail: achapman@swmedctr.com
www.swmedctr.com
Pages 140-143

Tapani Underground
1904 SE 6th Place
PO Box 1900
Battle Ground, Washington 98604
Phone: 360-687-1148
Fax: 360-687-7968
E-mail: tapaniund@juno.com
Page 134

Tidewater Barge Lines, Inc.
PO Box 1210
Vancouver, Washington 98666-1210
Phone: 360-693-1491
Fax: 360-694-8981
E-mail: info@tidewater.com
www.tidewater.com
Pages 98-99

Underwriters Laboratories Inc. of Camas
2600 NW Lake Road
Camas, Washington 98607
Phone: 360-817-5500
Fax: 360-817-6000
E-mail: camas@ul.com
www.ul.com
Pages 110-111

Vancouver Business Journal
2525 E 4th Plain Boulevard
Vancouver, Washington 98661
Phone: 360-695-2442
Fax: 360-695-3056
E-mail: publisher@vbjusa.com
www.vbjusa.com
Page 104

The Vancouver Clinic
700 NE 87th Avenue
Vancouver, Washington 98664
Phone: 360-254-1240
Fax: 360-256-9216
Page 145

WaferTech
5509 NW Parker Street
Camas, Washington 98607
Phone: 360-817-3000
Fax: 360-817-3590
www.wafertech.com
Page 114

Wendel Family Dental Centre
7012 NE 40th Street
Vancouver, Washington 98661
Phone: 360-254-5254
Fax: 360-254-3698
E-mail: mail@wendeldental.com
www.wendeldental.com
Page 144

West Coast Bank
801 Main Street
Vancouver, Washington 98660
Phone: 360-695-3439
Fax: 360-693-5667
www.wcb.com
Page 126

Bibliography

Brokaw, Tom. *The Greatest Generation*. New York: Random House, 1998.

Chamberlain, Holly, and Kubik, Barbara. *Clark County Historic Survey and Inventory Report* (submitted to the Washington State Office of Archaeology and Historic Preservation, September 28, 1999, by Heritage Research Associates, Inc., Robert Freed, project manager). Vancouver, Washington: Clark County Historic Preservation Commission, 1999.

Dietrich, William. *Northwest Passage: The Great Columbia River*. New York: Simon & Schuster, 1995.

Harper, J. Russell. *Paul Kane's Frontier*. Austin: University of Texas Press, 1971.

Jollota, Pat. "Clark County History." In *Vancouver & Southwest Washington Visitor and Relocation Guide*. Vancouver Business Journal, 1997.

Lamb, W. Kaye, ed. *The Voyage of George Vancouver (1791-1795)*, Vol II. London: The Hakluyt Society, 1984.

Nokes, J. Richard. *Almost a Hero: The Voyages of John Meares, R.N., to China, Hawaii and the Northwest Coast*. Pullman: Washington State University Press, 1998.

Rose, Mary, and Van Arsdol, Ted. *U.S. Army Vancouver Barracks: Northwest's Oldest Military Post*. Vancouver: The Columbian, January 24 - May 9, 1999.

Rubin, Rick. *Naked Against the Rain: The People of the Lower Columbia River, 1770-1830*. Portland, Oregon: Far Shore Press, 1999.

Van Arsdol, Ted. *Vancouver on the Columbia: An Illustrated History*. Foreword by Milton Bona. Northridge, California: Windsor Publications, 1986.

Wulff, Jane Elder. *Bugle Call: Early Days at Vancouver Barracks* (unpublished fictional memoir based on historical research for fourth grade curriculum, "A Visit to Officers Row"). Vancouver, Washington: City of Vancouver, Office of Heritage Services, 1996.

Wulff, Jane Elder. *Heritage Resource Directory*. Vancouver: Heritage Trust of Clark County, 1994.

Index

Academy at St. James Cathedral, 54
Air Museum in the Murdock Aviation Center, 55
Albright, Madeleine, 77
American Institute of Architects, 30
Army's Department of the Columbia, 38
Association for Portland Progress, 40

Bacon, Tony, 41
baseball, 66
Battle Ground School District, 33, 152
Battle Ground Reflector, 58
Battle Ground's Rose Float, 67
Bear Paw Mountains, 87
Big Doctor, 46
Bi-State Transportation Committee, 77
Boise Cascade, 112-113
Bonneville Power Administration, 24, 96-97
Brokaw, Tom, 77
Broughton, Lieutenant William, 17, 45-46
Buffalo Soldiers, 47
Burdick, Steve, 30, 38
Burnt Bridge Creek, 47

Camas School District, 152
Canby, General E.R.S., 38
Cascades, 75,
Celebrate Freedom, 77
Center for Agriculture, Science, and Environmental Education, 33, 54
Central Park, 38, 66
Century 21 Complete Realty, 133
Chatham, 46
Chkalov, Valeri P., 55
Chief Joseph, 87
Chinook, 16, 19, 46, 63
City of Vancouver's Office of Neighborhood Services, 48
Civil War, 38
Clark College, 25, 29, 31, 34, 67, 150-151
Clark County, 11, 15, 21, 24, 26, 30-31, 33-34, 37, 40, 45, 47-48, 50, 54-55, 57-58, 63, 65-69, 74-78, 83-84, 87
Clark County Fair, 68-69
Clark County School Employees Credit Union, 129
Clark County Skills Center, 33
Clark, William, 21
Columbia Credit Union, 122-123
Columbia District, 18
Columbia Land Trust, 55, 87
Columbia Rediviva, 17, 22
Columbia River, 15-16, 18-19, 21-22, 30, 38, 42, 45, 71, 73, 75, 87, 89
Columbia River Education and Workforce Council, 30
Columbia River Economic Development Council, 30
Columbia River Renaissance, 18, 21, 38
ConAgra Malt: Great Western Malting Company, 116
Corps of Discovery, 21, 64, 89
Covington, Richard and Ann, 30

Daughters of the British Empire, 17
Dearborn, Steve, 84, 87
Demetro, Christina, 11, 16
Demetro, Eva, 11, 16
Demetro, Jim, 16-17, 89
DePreist, James, 77
Design Showroom, Inc., 127
Discovery Walk Festival, 64

Economic Development Services for the City of Vancouver, 30
Educational Service District 112, 30, 152
Elks Lodge, 68
Elliott, Bob, 76
Esther Short Park, 40-41, 48, 66, 86-87
Evergreen School District, 33, 152
Evergreen Hotel, 87

Fair Housing Act, 47
Farmer, Grace, 48
fireworks, Fourth of July, 68
Ford Foundation Innovations in Government award, 30
Fort Lewis, 38
Fort Vancouver Historical Society, 56
Fort Vancouver National Historic Site, 54, 78
Fort Vancouver Regional Library System, 34
Fort Vancouver, 18-19, 34, 46-47, 54-56, 63, 67, 74-75, 78, 89
Frenchman's Bar, 39
Frichtl, Dianne, 40
Friends of Vancouver, 16
Fromhold, Bill, 11, 40

General George C. Marshall Public Service Leadership Award, 77
George C. Marshall Lecture Series, 77
Gifford Pinchot National Forest, 66
golf, 40, 66
Gorton, Slade, 38
Grant House Folk Art Center, 65
Grant House, 21, 38, 65
Grant, Ulysses S., 38, 54

Gray, Captain Robert, 17
Greater Vancouver Chamber of Commerce, 40, 77, 83-84, 120-121
Green Mountain School District, 32, 152
Growth Management Plan, 40, 84

Habitat Partners, 55
Harvest Days Parade, 67
Hasart, Dr. Tana, 31
Hatheway, Major John, 46
Hickey, Ray, 58
Hicks, Tim, 54
Hidden, Lowell, 30
Hockinson School District, 153
Holland Restaurant, 67
Hough, Paddy, 54
House of Providence, 30
Howard, General Oliver O., 87
Hudson's Bay Company, 18-19, 30, 46
Hudson's Bay High School, 77

Identity Clark County, 40
"I Have A Dream" Foundation, 57
International Marching League, 64

Jefferson, Thomas, 21
Johnson, Leann, 47
Jollota, Pat, 47

Kaiser Permanente, 57, 146
Kane, Paul, 74, 77
Kassab, Elie, 16, 40
Katz, Vera, 77
Killian Pacific, 136
KVAN radio, 58
Kyocera Industrial Ceramics Corporation, 115

La Center, 56, 67
La Center School District, 153
Lacamas Community Credit Union, 128
Lady Washington, 22
Larson, Jim, 68
Le Slam Sports Bar, 67
Lewis and Clark Bicentennial, 87
Lewis and Clark, 64, 87
Lewis, Meriwether, 21, 84
LSW Architects, P.C., 124-125

magnet schools, 33
Marshall Elementary School, 77
Marshall House, 21, 38, 58
Marshall, General George C., 38, 54-55, 77
Marshall, John, 58, 87
Massey, Avril, 17
Matthias, Mark, 67
McFarland, Sharon, 30
McLoughlin, John, 30, 46
Metropolitan Greenspaces Program, 77
Mill Plain Boulevard Extension, 39, 84
Mother Joseph, 30
Mount St. Helens, 74-75, 77
Murdock, Jack, 55
Musser, Tom, 68

National Historic Reserve, 20-21, 39-40, 54, 77, 87
National League of Cities, 48
National Public Radio, 67
National Waterfront Center, 18
Neighborhood Outreach program, 48
New Edge Networks, 102-103
Nez Perce, 83, 87, 89
Norris, Beggs & Simpson, 132
North Coast Electric Company, 135
North County Community Food Bank, 58
Northwest Passage, 21, 46
Northwest Surgical Specialists, 57
Northwest, 16, 21, 24, 30, 38-39, 46, 57, 66-67
NUSA Notable by Neighborhoods USA, 48

Officers Row, 20-21, 38, 40, 42, 47, 54, 58, 77
Old Apple Tree Park, 46
Oregon Department of Environmental Quality, 76
Oregon Symphony, 77
Oregon Territory, 46
Oregon Trade Language, 46
Oregon, 18, 22, 46, 76-77
Otak, 136

paper mills, 18
Parsley, Dr. James, 32
Pearson Field, 55
Pearson Jr., Lieutenant Alexander, 55
Phelps, Kelly Joe, 67
Point Vancouver, 21, 46
Pollard, Royce, 17, 22, 73, 77, 87
Pomeroy Living History Farm, 18, 56
Portland, 18, 22, 40-41, 57, 66-67, 73, 75-78

Portland Art Museum, 78
Portland Rose Festival Parade, 67
Portland Trail Blazers, 57, 78
Portland Winter Hawks, 66
Powell, General Colin L., 77
Propstra Field, 66
Propstra, George and Carolyn, 58
Punteney, Kelly, 39

railroads, 18, 56
Ray Hickey: Hickey Family Company, 100-101
Redheart, 87
Responsible Growth Forum, 40
Ridgefield National Wildlife Refuge, 65
Ridgefield School District, 153
River of the West, 17
Rockies, 21, 74

sawmills, 18
schools, 25, 30-33, 40, 48, 54-55, 84
Sharp, 27, 41, 108-109
Sherman, General William Tecumseh, 38
shipbuilding, 18
shipping, 18
Silver Star Range, 66
Simpson, Sir George, 46
skiing, 67
Slevoire Hall, 54
Southwest Clean Air Agency, 76
Southwest Washington Child Care Consortium, 30
Southwest Washington Medical Center, 26, 57, 140
St. Joseph's Sausage Festival, 67
Steam Team #539, 56
Stroganoff family art collection, 78

Tapani Underground, 134
Tears of Joy Puppet Theatre, 67
"The Friendly Reach," 46, 48
Tidewater Barge Lines, Inc., 58, 98-99

U.S. Fish & Wildlife Service, 87
U.S.S. *Massachusetts*, 46
Underwriters Laboratories Inc. of Camas, 110-111

VA hospital, 38
Vancouver Barracks, 38-39, 47, 54, 65, 83, 87, 89
Vancouver Business Journal, 58, 104
Vancouver, Captain George, 16-17, 22, 38, 46, 90
Vancouver Clinic, The, 145
Vancouver Columbian, 30, 53, 57-58
Vancouver District, 32
Vancouver Farmer's Market, 65, 87
Vancouver Housing Authority, 47
Vancouver Lake, 39, 55, 65-66
Vancouver National Historic Reserve Trust, 20-21, 39, 54, 77, 87
Vancouver Public Schools, 153
Vancouver Symphony Orchestra, 67
Vancouver's Fourth of July celebration, 67
Veterans Day Parade, 67, 70, 77

WaferTech, 114
Walkable Community Awards, 65
Walking magazine, 65
Wapato Lowlands, 16
Washington, Kermit, 67
Washington State School for the Deaf, 33, 153
Washington State School for the Blind, 33, 153
Washington State University, 31
Washougal School District, 153
Water Resources Education Center, 39, 55, 60, 65
Wendel Family Dental Centre, 144
West Coast Bank, 126
whitewater rivers, 67
Willamette, 18
Wine & Jazz Festival, 67

YMCA, 66
Yoder, Ray, 32
YWCA's Diversity Task Force, 47

*A special thanks to the following patrons
for their support of* **Vancouver: A Portrait of Prosperity**

AXCYL Incorporated

Aztec International Timber & Trading, Ltd.

City of Vancouver Water Resources Education Center

NW Natural Gas

Vancouver Warehouse & Distribution Co.